SPINNING DISNEY'S WORLD

SPINNING DISNEY'S WORLD

*Memories of a
Magic Kingdom Press Agent*

Charles Ridgway

SPINNING DISNEY'S WORLD
MEMORIES OF A MAGIC KINGDOM PRESS AGENT

Published by The Intrepid Traveler, P.O. Box 531, Branford, CT 06405
www.intrepidtraveler.com

First Edition
Printed in Canada
Cover design by Foster & Foster
Interior design by Alfonso Robinson
ISBN: 1-887140-67-0
ISBN 13: 978-1-887140-67-6
Library of Congress Control Number: 2006928897
Distributed to the trade by National Book Network

9 8 7 6 5 4 3 2 1 hardcover

Photo Credits

Dedication

To my wife, Gretta, who shared fifty-three magical years with me, and my children, Janet and Scott, who continue to enrich my life after Disney.

Foreword

Forty years of playing press agent for Walt Disney's Mouse Houses on three continents has given me a mental library of "war stories" about Walt himself and his "Imagineers" plus visiting showbiz stars and behind the scenes tales of publicizing the world's most famous outdoor entertainment parks — tales I enjoyed telling to my news media friends for many years.

They were the ones who suggested putting the stories in writing. Translating these verbal tales to the printed page would be easier if I could do it with a wink and a smile.

Starting as a Disneyland publicity writer, I soon developed a secondary specialty setting up photographs of visitors and special events — including telling Walt Disney himself where to stand when he was part of the setup. Not too many tried telling Walt where to go.

My favorite picture was the last one we shot of Walt in 1966 — sitting on a bright red fire engine beside Mickey Mouse in front of Sleeping Beauty Castle at Disneyland. Both are smiling. It was shot by my friend and co-worker Charlie Nichols, but I was the one who got to tell Walt where to sit.

That picture, used thousands of times since, really captures the essence of Walt Disney for me — happiness, memories and fantasies.

Since I began my working life as a reporter and writer, the best part of my Disney job was meeting thousands of fellow journalists from magazines, radio, television and newspapers around the world — entertaining them and being a guide for their family visits to Disney parks in Florida, California, France and Hong Kong. Many were internationally known writers and broadcasters, fascinating to know.

Making friends with them was vital to my job. I went to see them in their offices. They came to see Mickey Mouse and the parks. We talked about their Disney experiences but even more we talked about ourselves — our families, our joys, our jobs, our troubles and ambitions, the state of the world.

Which is where these tales were first told. Some are funny. Some are sad, full of miscues and triumphs. Some are even unbelievable. Hopefully they reveal some of the magic that Walt Disney's world has brought to my life and the lives of millions of people, ordinary and mighty, around the world.

Chapter I

$\mathcal{T}$here I was, less than a week into my new press agent's job at Disneyland, standing on top of a desk to reach photo files on shelves that stretched up to a fifteen-foot Victorian ceiling. It was Monday, the park was closed; there was no one around. The year was 1963, January. The door opened behind me.

"May we come in?" inquired an unseen voice.

"Hell, yes," I said. "It's not my joint."

But it was *his*. This was Disneyland's City Hall Police Station and that was Walt Disney himself followed by his staff on a typical "walk-through."

I said, "Hello," too embarrassed to look at his face to see whether Walt was amused or annoyed. The group took a fast look around the tiny office, packed to the gills with all the Publicity Department's press releases, fact sheets and photos ready for hand-out or mail-out to writers and editors for newspapers and magazines across the country.

Perhaps intimidated by the clutter of an office barely large enough for two desks, mine and my secretary's, and a wall full of shelves, the "inspectors" left quickly without comment or conversation other than Walt's hurried "Thanks."

Thus began, less than auspiciously, a forty-year career as a publicist for Disney parks in California, Florida, France and, most recently, Hong Kong. This was the first of many times I saw Walt striding across Town Square at the head of his management team — always walking fast and always ahead.

❦

My love of Disneyland began much earlier — even before the invitational celebrity/press preview July 17, 1955. As a reporter for the *Los Angeles Mirror-News*, I first became intrigued watching strange hills, buildings and rivers take shape as I drove down Harbor Boulevard in 1954.

For months I tried to get my city editor/boss, Hank Osborne, to let me do a picture feature on it. Our tabloid paper was big on pictures.

"Wait until it's nearer done," he kept saying.

Finally, in April, 1955, he got tired of my pestering and gave me the go ahead. My hook for the story was "An Anaheim kid sneaks into Disneyland under the construction fence for a preview look." Disneyland Publicity Manager Eddie Meck wasn't too thrilled with the idea because he could visualize every kid in town trying to repeat the maneuver. But he let me try it.

Since I had no children at the time, I borrowed a neighbor, five-year-old David Potthast, as my model.

Mirror-News photographer Delmar Watson met us at the construction gate. Delmar and his brothers — five of them — were famous among L.A. photographers as slightly nutty and full of gags. All of them had appeared in *Our Gang* comedies and other movies as child actors (the best known was Bobs Watson). Delmar had also scored as a child comedian and carried his comedic talents into his photographic career. He always carried crazy props just in case — things like a beat-up Boy Scout hat, oversized rubber boots, a battered bugle, even a fishing pole. We used them all.

We posed David in his "seven league boots, arms akimbo" in front of a half-finished Sleeping Beauty Castle. We had him fishing off the dock in Frontierland — no water in the river. In fact, the first time they filled the river it was dry by the next morning. It took weeks to line it with a hard clay to keep water in.

David was one of those kids we used to call spunky — always in some kind of devilment with a wicked little gleam in his eyes. He made a perfect model. We took his picture leaning out the window of a stagecoach (no horses), climbing a man-made rock in Adventureland and, of course, crawling under the fence.

As we went around I noticed several #6 flash bulbs lying around and got suspicious. I called the city desk to tell them I thought another newspaper was working on the story and suggested I come in and write it for the next day. Delmar was already on the way with his photos.

"We're too tight tomorrow. Wait and write it Monday and we'll get it in next week."

Monday morning, the *Los Angeles Examiner* came out with a double-truck of pictures detailing progress on the Disneyland construction site. I'm still mad about getting beat on "my story."

The capper, however, came Monday afternoon when David Potthast's mother got a call from his kindergarten teacher to come in for a conference.

"David is a wonderful little boy," the teacher began. "And we really encourage imagination, but he came to school today with a completely unbelievable story. He may need psychiatric help. He claims he sneaked into Disneyland and went fishing, rode a stagecoach and posed in front of the castle *and* he refused to admit he was making it up."

Poor David, he spent the entire day under a cloud of suspicion, all because he went to Disneyland. He won in the end, however, when his pictures appeared with my story three days later.

The story appeared May 5, 1955. Exactly fifty years to the day later, I was on hand for the beginning of Disneyland's year-long fiftieth anniversary.

I was one of many reporters who covered the invitational celebrity/press preview day on July 17, 1955. I claim I may be the only person who had a thoroughly wonderful time that day.

The park was barely ready, the day was boiling hot, many of the rides broke down and a crowd of twenty-eight thousand, twice the number invited, completely overwhelmed employees' ability to feed, guide and entertain them. It was forever known as "Black Sunday" by Disneylanders.

Women's high heels sank into the overheated blacktop on Main Street, a gas leak caused evacuation of one area for a time and guests were moved out of the way to make room for gigantic television cameras broadcasting the event *live*. There were no lines, just mob scenes in front of each attraction as people fought to climb aboard the *Jungle Cruise* boats, the steam train, or the "dark rides" in Fantasyland. When rides broke down, even temporarily, tempers flared.

My friend Milt Albright, who headed Disneyland Group Sales, told a typical unreported tale. He was assigned to take a state senator around the park. They were sitting on the deck of the steamboat *Mark Twain* when a window frame fell out and crashed over the senator's head. That's the way to impress them, Milt!

The all-live-they-didn't-have-tape-in-those-days television show of the event was full of glitches. Anchorman Hank Weaver called for a report from Ronald Reagan in Tomorrowland and wound up talking with actor Bob Cummings in Frontierland. Restaurants ran out of food and were down to serving a slab of cheese on a slice of bread by early afternoon. Most of the overheated crowd with crying kids and sunburned faces left early.

But I had a ball. Because I lived only a few blocks away, I arrived, to the annoyance of Eddie Meck and his all-new publicity staff, way too early, at nine instead of the expected noontime. At least I missed the horrendous traffic jam coming down Firestone Boulevard from Los Angeles. The Santa Ana Freeway didn't extend that far at the time.

My wife, Gretta, had a new aqua and white linen dress with matching shoes for the occasion. Despite the heat, I wore a navy sport coat. It was a dress-up affair. As I pinned on a blue ribbon that said "Working Press Pass, Disneyland Preview, July 17" (no year noted) we spotted Walt on the upper level of the train station pointing out a missed spot to a painter frantically trying to finish before the crowd arrived.

I checked in at the Press Tent, in a backstage parking lot, and stumbled over chubby TV cables that ran in every direction to each of the five lands. Television-studio-size cameras were on hand to transmit pictures of all the activities. No little hand-held ENG — electronic news gathering — tape cameras in those days!

I picked up press releases and fact sheets, then walked down to Sleeping Beauty Castle where Walt was rehearsing commercials. He was nervous as a mouse — not Mickey! — flubbing lines and running his fingers through his hair.

We wandered into Frontierland where Fess Parker and sidekick Buddy Ebsen on horseback were rehearsing their Davy Crockett bit and saw Irene Dunne getting instructions on champagne bottle breaking across the bow of the stern wheel steamboat *Mark Twain*.

Attractions were not open until noon. Tomorrowland was largely undone, and Fantasyland was closed off behind a raised drawbridge waiting for the kids of Anaheim to race across it on cue when it was lowered later in the day.

Many Los Angeles business writers had said Disneyland was bound to be a colossal failure.

"Why," they asked, "would Walt go way out there in the middle of nowhere and fool around with an amusement park when such parks were dying all over the country?"

And when other operators heard Walt planned to charge *admission* ($1.50) in addition to selling tickets (10¢ to 50¢) for each attraction, well, the experts said, that just wasn't done.

Many of Walt's studio employees, I heard, resented the fact that the boss was wasting all this time and money in Anaheim when "he should be back in Hollywood making movies." Some were still jealous nine years later when the park made more money than the movies for the first time.

The new park was originally planned for a site just across Riverside Drive from the Walt Disney Studios in Burbank. The area was quite small. Walt had to look elsewhere when city planners balked at anticipated traffic problems and he discovered he needed a much larger site for his ideas. I had heard about the traffic stymie from a news contact at L.A. City Hall even before I heard anything about the park.

Anaheim was picked after a study by Stanford Research showed land available at what would be the center of Southern California's future growth. Walt and his brother, Roy O. Disney, originally planned to spend about $4 million.

At the end of six months they had committed $11 million and hocked everything they had, including life insurance policies and homes. They arranged participant sponsorships on attractions like the *Santa Fe & Disneyland Railroad* and with Richfield Oil Company for the *Autopia*. They sold leases on shops, including some to friends of Walt like Art Linkletter. They were still $6 million short.

Walt went to the ABC-TV network, the same ABC that Disney bought forty years later, which agreed to underwrite a $4.5 million loan in return for a piece of the park and outdoor food concessions. ABC didn't care about the park. They wanted Walt to produce a weekly TV show called *Disneyland* at a time when major studios in Hollywood were boycotting TV and not allowing their stars to appear on the new medium.

In fact, when I began work as a reporter in L.A. in 1952, TV news crews were forced to wait outside political press conferences until newspaper reporters finished asking questions. Imagine TV reporters putting up with that today! One paper had a rule that any reporter who appeared in even one shot on TV was automatically fired.

Walt knew that his TV shows would sell his new park across the country. He began airing his *Disneyland* ten months before the park opened, pretending to be originating it from locations like Fantasyland, Frontierland, Adventureland, and Tomorrowland.

Back in Town Square on that press preview day, I watched cameramen rehearsing locations for the flag-raising, when California Governor Goodwin Knight and other dignitaries would join Walt in opening ceremonies on TV.

Because of the *Disneyland* television shows, expectations were clear over the top all across the nation as well as among those all-too-many thousands who turned up for opening day. Park operations tried to explain the mix-up, claiming someone had been counterfeiting tickets for the preview.

I have my own theory but can't get anyone to confirm it. Invitations were sent to a long list of Hollywood celebrities and Walt's friends, plus L.A. editors, photographers and reporters like me, plus all those construction workers with families who had been promised an invite if they got the park finished on time.

The invitation read, "You and your family are invited ..." and enclosed an RSVP card to list the number of people in your family and reply to the invitation. "Tickets" then were mailed back, one for each member of the family. But that ticket also read, "You and your family are invited ..." Well, many recipients gave the "extra" tickets to neighbors, friends, and their favorite plumber who then came presenting their "family" ticket to gain admission for their whole group.

As the crowd began to grow, Gretta and I waited in Town Square watching Danny Thomas, Debbie Reynolds and beau Eddie Fisher and many other celebrities arriving along with an overeager vanguard of the crowd to come. The celebs included Frank Sinatra, Jerry Lewis, Sammy Davis Jr., and Buddy Ebsen. Press included columnist Hedda Hopper and entertainment editors and movie critics from all the L.A. papers as well as managing editors, city editors and many more. Many of Walt's best friends in Hollywood, directors, producers, actors and agents also came to show their support for what many called "Walt's Folly!"

"We'd better get something to eat," I told Gretta around 11:30 a.m., "It's really going to be crowded."

We found a prime spot on the verandah at the Red Wagon Inn, Swift Premium's best in-park restaurant, and had a great prime-rib dinner. We overheard Eddie Fisher telling how they had a flat tire on the way to the park and he had to wait while Debbie changed the tire. That was a joke, I guess.

By the time we were through, Main Street, U.S.A. was packed. Gretta gave up and went home, figuring she could easily come another day. I retired to the press tent and watched television sets that were turned on for rehearsals. I could see it better from there. Early in the afternoon I went back to Town Square to watch the dedication.

"To all who come to this happy place, welcome. Disneyland is your land. Here age relives fond memories of the past and here youth may savor the challenge and promise of the future.

Disneyland is dedicated to the ideals, the dreams and the hard facts which have created America ...with the hope that it will be a source of joy and inspiration to the world."

July 17, 1955

Those were Walt's words as he unveiled a temporary cardboard plaque later replaced by one in bronze. It was many years before I understood the full significance of those words. At the time, I went back to the press tent to watch the rest of the show while other reporters and photographers covered the action in other areas.

I missed seeing Walt driving the steam train or Ward Kimball and his Firehouse Five Plus Two Dixieland Band riding atop the *Santa Fe & Disneyland Steam Railroad* freight train all afternoon of that Disneyland Preview day.

About five o'clock, I wandered onto Main Street and discovered the place was almost deserted. The intense heat of the afternoon that drove the crowd away was giving way to an ocean breeze. I phoned Gretta.

"Come back! We can go on everything."

Orange County reporter Dorothy Fisher, who was hired to help in Publicity for the opening, went with us. We rode on the *Jungle Cruise, Snow White's Adventure*, the *Santa Fe & Disneyland Railroad*, the *Mark Twain* steamboat and more, many of which had broken down earlier. No waiting. It was just plain fun.

I was shocked when I read our *Mirror-News* reports on Monday afternoon. Like other papers, the stories concentrated on all the negatives — the heat, the crowds, the frustration, the breakdowns, but said little about what was working. Columnists complained about such things as the lack of drinking fountains, theorizing that Walt was trying to make people drink Coca Cola.

The truth was, plumbers came to Walt not long before opening and gave him a choice of fountains or toilets. Seems he chose toilets — always the practical type.

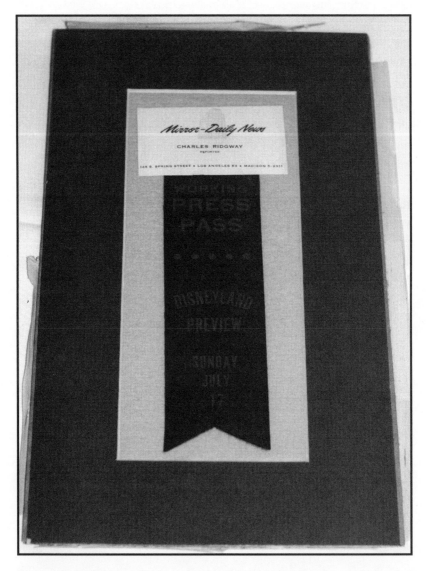

My press badge from the official opening day of Disneyland is one of my most cherished possessions. Wonder how much it would fetch on eBay?

Chapter 2

The press had said, "Stay away. It's not finished. It's too crowded."

So, naturally, the public rushed out to see what all the hullaba-loo was about. A comfortable crowd of ten thousand paying guests came out on Monday. Park operators soon discovered that they had to limit attendance to about twenty thousand to avoid overcrowd-ing during the busy summer ahead.

More than a million guests came through the gates in the first seven weeks — *Phenomenal!* — proving the nay-sayers were wrong again. The park soon became known around the world as a place where show-business celebrities and millions of ordinary people went for something new and different.

Still, Walt and Disneyland managers were shocked by the press reaction and immediately began a campaign of inviting all the press guests back, a few at a time. Many were taken on personal tours by Walt himself.

To cope with the crowds, park managers began dispersing the mob at ticket windows and installing ropes to create orderly waits. The line for the *Jungle Cruise* ran double file for three blocks clear back to the Main Street Train Station before the Disney hosts dis-covered they could weave roped aisles to turn the mob into an or-derly procession still within sight of the attraction. Walt had re-membered similar queues at London theaters. He put in musical groups and other entertainers to keep guests amused while wait-ing.

But at the end of the summer, the kids went back to school and during the fall of 1955 the park was near empty on many days. The rainiest fall in twenty years didn't help either. It began to look like the early success was a summer romance gone sour. Many weekdays saw fewer than a thousand guests on hand. Lessees from the shops formed the Disneyland Merchants Association and began complaining.

Seeking to boost attendance, Walt installed a circus in the unfinished area of Tomorrowland, hired acrobats, clowns and animals. He named it the *Mickey Mouse Club Circus* and brought cast members from his new children's television show to star. The *Mickey Mouse Club*, Walt's first TV program for kids, had gone on the air in October.

Stars like Annette, Cubby, Karen, Bobby, Jimmie Dodd and long-time Disney cartoonist Big Roy Williams were an immediate success on TV and helped boost attendance, but still not enough to satisfy the park's needs. Only later did Walt realize that people would rather ride the Disney adventures instead of sitting in a show of any kind.

The circus also created some amusing operational problems. Retired Admiral Joseph Fowler, head of Disneyland construction, spent an hour chasing a wayward circus goat down the *Santa Fe & Disneyland Railroad* tracks. He talked about it for years.

Joe Fowler, a legendary figure in Disney history and later chairman of the Disneyland Operating Committee, was one of the most interesting "characters" who ever wandered through the park. His forty years of Disney service didn't even begin until his middle age retirement from an illustrious career as a naval architect and shipyard commander in the U.S. Navy. He had retired a second time after mapping a whole new organizational plan for the Armed Forces. He was known by everyone as the "can do" man.

When Walt, as he frequently did, asked the *impossible*, Joe's stock answer was, "Can do." Fowler, as head of construction, was the man most responsible for building Disneyland, and later. Walt

Disney World's Magic Kingdom park. Disney Imagineers designed it. Admiral Fowler built it. Joe loved to tell how he came to work for Walt when Disneyland construction was just starting.

Fowler lived in Northern California when Walt first heard about him as an expert marine architect and went to see him in 1954 to talk about building the steamboat *Mark Twain.* Joe agreed to come down to Burbank and take a look at the plans.

A few days later, with only a briefcase and an extra shirt, he arrived at the Disney Studios expecting to stay only one day. Walt showed him the beginning of the riverboat on a Studio backlot.

"How'd you like to come and help me build Disneyland?" Walt asked.

I guess Joe's answer must have been "can do," because after they talked a little longer Walt excused himself to go to a movie story conference and told Joe, "See my secretary, she will show you to your office."

It was three weeks before the Admiral was even able to go home for fresh clothes.

And he was on hand throughout the months of building Disneyland in 1954 and '55 and indeed until well into the 1980s when he was still advising the Imagineers.

That was typical of how Walt picked his key people.

As I said, in the fall of 1955 things were not going well. On a Friday afternoon you could shoot a pop-gun down Main Street and not hit anyone. Payroll checks were still hand-written and on occasion salaried employees were asked to wait until Monday to cash them — until the busier weekend receipts were deposited.

Managers recommended Walt close for the off-season and re-open during summers and holidays. He refused.

"I don't want the place run by a bunch of seasonal itinerants," he said.

Earlier, his personnel manager had planned to hire people with experience in running carnivals or amusement parks.

"No way," Walt said.

"But we don't know anything about running an amusement park," was the reply.

"I don't care, we'll hire bright young people and teach them our way," Walt said. "We'll make mistakes, but we will learn to do it better than anyone. Besides it is *not* an amusement park."

Early on, someone put coin slots on toilet stall doors without telling Walt, but he soon got rid of that, along with carny types hawking programs at the front gate. This definitely was *not* an amusement park.

When his first general manager began claiming credit for building the park, Walt soon changed things, fired the offender, and vowed never to make that mistake again. He created a Park Operating Committee composed of the director of each division — operations, marketing, maintenance, corporate participants, entertainment and so forth. That committee, with rotating chairmen, made the plans and ran the day-to-day operation and still does.

In those days in the entire Disney company, there was only Roy O. Disney as President, and a vice-president of finance — no other vice-presidents anywhere. Walt held no corporate office — he didn't want to have to waste time signing all those papers. In today's Disney operations, vice-presidents are as thick as fleas on a hound dog. But they would have had a hard time when Walt was there. There was never a doubt who was boss. It was Walt.

In the first year, Walt wandered the park, particularly on weekends, talking with guests, looking for ways to improve everything. No detail was too small to catch his attention.

Walt's management style was totally different from that of most of today's big corporations. He knew exactly what would make the public happy and had supreme confidence in his ability to make the right choices. He worked long, hard hours and expected as much from all those around him. He noticed every detail. Those who stayed — Imagineers, filmmakers and even publicists like me — would do every thing we could, gladly, just to please Walt. He walked fast and expected everyone to keep up.

Many of the early hires were college students who returned to school in the fall, but they returned for vacations, summers and holidays, when they were most needed. By and large they came from well-educated middle-class families. This was their first job. Many stayed on to become full time cast members just because they loved working there.

Among the early hires was Ron Dominguez, who was born in a red-tiled house in the middle of the orange groves that Walt bought for his park. He stayed for forty years, eventually becoming head of Disneyland operations. Dick Nunis, who began as a trainer of ride operators, wound up as chairman of all the Disney parks before re-tiring nearly fifty years later. The Dominguez family home, which served as an all-too-small park headquarters for the first ten years, was where I went for my job interview. Un-air-conditioned sheds attached to each end served as store rooms for the operations and marketing department.

I realized Disneyland was really something special months be-fore its opening. Oddly, I was the only reporter on any of the L.A. metropolitan newspapers to live in Orange County. I moved to Anaheim, almost by accident, in 1953 when it was a quiet little town of nineteen thousand people. "Lum and Abner" still ran the local hardware store stocked with all those old fashioned things they had ordered during the war but didn't get until peace came.

The SQR Department Store still moved its cash from counter to counting house on the mezzanine in little wire cages that trav-eled on ropes and pulleys. There was a Chinese restaurant on Main Street, a hamburger café with great shoestring potatoes nearby and a barbeque steak house out on the highway, Firestone Boulevard, but that was it when it came to fancy eating. None of those build-ings remain. All were torn down to make room for a big-city down-town.

The small house we bought for $13,750 in the town's second real estate subdivision was way on the edge of town, at least twelve blocks from the center of town. But that was before Disneyland. The town has grown so much that our house "on the edge of town" is now fifteen miles from the present-day city limits. Anaheim's 1953 population was about twenty thousand, less than one fourth the number of people who now visit Disneyland in a busy day.

Telephoning from Anaheim to Santa Ana was a long distance call, a fact that resulted in many midnight wake-up calls for me from off-duty Marines at local taverns. Seems the number for the El Toro Marine Air Station in Santa Ana was the same as mine except for the area code. So if the Marines dialed it as a local call from their favorite Anaheim cocktail lounge without operator assistance, they got me.

"Tell the O.D. I'll be late for reveille," was the favorite message. I got tired of arguing, so I replied, "Yessir, I'll tell him." Sure glad the town grew up.

Because I lived near the park during those early years, I was frequently assigned by the *Los Angeles Mirror-News* to cover events such as the Junior Ambassadors program, an international children's congress picked by Disney offices around the world and flown for meetings at Disneyland. Celebrities from Hollywood and Broadway and government leaders came, including President Sukarno of Indonesia, the first of many heads of state to make official visits. Most notable were Prime Minister Nehru of India, the Crown Prince and Princess of Japan (with a mob of photographers) and Presidents Eisenhower, Truman and Kennedy. Walt frequently drove the celebrities himself in an electric horseless carriage.

With Nehru, a careful itinerary was laid out with Secret Service approval, but as Walt was driving around the castle hub, he suddenly told Nehru, "I want to show you my newest ride," and turned in a totally unplanned direction, leaving press and Secret Service trying to catch up.

Of course, the most famous "visitor" was the one who didn't get to go — Soviet Premier Nikita Khrushchev. Touring Hollywood, Khrushchev was told about Disneyland by Frank Sinatra on the set of *Can-Can*. He told his official hosts he wanted to visit Walt's park. The mayor of Los Angeles and Police Chief William Parker, showing a decided lack of hospitality for "communists," told the Russian security men they could not guarantee his security for such a trip, never pointing out that it wasn't their job but would be handled by State Police, the Orange County Sheriff and Disneyland security. There is probably no safer place for a celebrity to go because of the park's controlled gates and carefully controlled environment. Khrushchev was so mad he pounded the desk with his shoe when he appeared at the U.N. later that month.

Disney publicity people at the time, who had been preparing for the visit for several days, were devastated by the missed opportunity. Yet his not going made headlines for years to come, probably far more than would have appeared if the visit had been made.

The first of the royal visitors I got to see was Emperor Haile Selassie of Ethiopia, who carried his little Chihuahua on his lap aboard the VIP electric carriage despite a park ruling against all but seeing-eye dogs.

After the *Mirror-News* folded at the end of 1961, I worked at the *Long Beach Press-Telegram* for a year as a feature writer roving around the Southland looking for good human interest stories — down at the beach, truck farms, the L.A. Harbor, wherever a good angle could be found. But when I was stuck, I always knew I could find a good personality feature at Disneyland. I got to know Publicity Manager Eddie Meck as a friend and news source.

When Eddie called to offer me a job as his one and only publicity writer, I thought about it long and hard. It was more money ($10 a week no less) than my $57 weekly reporter's salary. But I had tried public relations one time for six months with a small PR agency in L.A. and hated it. I thought we spent more trying to justify our work to clients than actually getting the job done. I had always planned to follow in my father's footsteps as a journalist.

But I decided if there were any publicity job in the world I could stomach for any length of time, this was it. Like most people, I was fascinated by Walt Disney himself. And the more I knew him, the more inspiring he became.

I had often seen and even talked with Walt as part of a group of newspeople during press conferences at the park, but never had a chance to meet face-to-face until that first time when he walked into my office at the City Hall Police Station.

I already had several friends among Disney people, including Eddie Meck and Joe Reddy, Walt's personal publicity rep. Both were old time Hollywood flacks. Eddie was a "planter" for the RKO Studios, which distributed Disney films, in the days when they sent reps to local newspapers to "plant" stories and pictures for the publicity department.

Joe was a former New York sportswriter — you know, the tough guy with a heart of gold type — who had been Shirley Temple's chief publicist. He used to bring the Disney "kids" to the courthouse in downtown Los Angeles for judges to approve their movie contracts. Of course he always brought them into the courthouse press room where I was working as a *Mirror-News* reporter so we could get their pictures — newcomers like Annette Funicello and the rest of the *Mickey Mouse Club* gang. Reporters from all five metropolitan papers shared the pressroom. We covered 105 courts with their celebrity divorces, murder trials and multi-million dollar civil suits, but we were always willing to call in the photographers for a shot of a pretty starlet or a cute kid.

Joe Reddy was the best of the publicists who came around, always ready with a new joke or a wild tale about scandalous behavior in Hollywood's good old days.

A small man with hair slicked close to his head, Eddie Meck had unusually large ears. San Francisco columnist Herb Caen used to refer to him lovingly as "Mecky Mouse." Eddie also knew how to make friends of newspeople by visiting with them, getting to know their likes and dislikes and those of their children and grandchildren. He made annual trips — always by train because of his fear of flying — to New York, Cleveland, Washington and Chicago. He spent hours on the phone and in person talking to editors and writers all over Southern California, which was our prime market.

Eddie needed a writer like me because he couldn't write a press release to save his life, but he had more good friends among newspaper and magazine reporters and editors than anyone I ever knew. He had known William Randolph Hearst's sons as kids running around the *Los Angeles Examiner's* city room when he was planting stories. He knew how reporters and editors thought and what they wanted. They all knew and liked Eddie. And he taught me all those things. They were the foundation for all of our press relations through the years.

The years that led up to my first Disney job were full of good fortune. My father was a newspaperman, Agricultural Editor of the *Chicago Tribune*, and one of the first graduates of the University of Missouri School of Journalism. Unlike a lot of kids who have trouble figuring out what they want to be when they grow up, I always knew I wanted to be a newsman. I think my Disney jobs were still a form of journalism because of the way we handled it. And I was able to keep writing about new things.

At MU, I worked on the student newspaper, created a local radio program of student news after World War II, and got involved in student government, where I was elected vice-president on a slate of fraternity members and independents. I was the independent rep. When the student body president decided to leave school in mid-year, I inherited his job, which is where I first learned the value of Eddie Meck's dictum — bring them to see for themselves.

In 1947, when Mizzou had grown from five thousand pre-war students to twenty thousand post-war with the advent of the GI Bill, there was a critical shortage of housing for students, many of whom were married by then. Musty wooden barracks from Fort

Leonard Wood had been brought up and planted on the University golf course. Students in the barracks ate at a makeshift cafeteria occupying the old ROTC building.

Our student government group, including a law student who later became governor of Missouri, went to President Middlebush (good name, huh?) asking for help.

"Not possible," was the answer. "We have been to the legislature. Only got half what we asked. No new dorms."

So we loaded into a car, trooped off to Jefferson City and bearded the Speaker of the House in his office. We advised him that he had twenty thousand voters (not to mention their parents) over in Columbia — not just some underage kids. And they were ready to revolt.

We got a long song and dance about the scarcity of money, a shortage of prison space and on and on. But the Speaker agreed to put together a delegation including the president of the Senate and come see for themselves.

We took them on a tour of the crowded, rat-infested and muddy-floored barracks, fed them dinner in the cafeteria on the same diet the students endured and took them to a basketball game where they were roundly booed.

Net result: the legislature that spring voted twice as much money as the University administration had requested, enough for many new dorms. The whole thing was written up in *Collier's* magazine after we left.

One final school note — when student election time came, we convinced a popular senior engineering student to run for president, assuring him that it would not interfere with his heavy load of school work. The next fall was when the University of Missouri decided to admit African-American students for the first time. Our chosen candidate spent hours on the phone with St. Louis newspapers and wire service reporters giving student opinion on the integration. I wonder if he ever had time to graduate.

❧

After college, I worked as a radio news reporter in central Illinois and Erie, Pennsylvania, before returning to newspaper work for a year on the *Erie Dispatch*. Figuring I needed to get to a larger city, and remembering how much I loved California when I was there as a GI in World War II, I took a chance. My wife and I made the move to L.A. with no job promises but a ray of hope from Ed Murray, the managing editor of the *Los Angeles Mirror*.

Ed made no promise but said if I came out, he would try to find a job for me sooner or later. It turned out to be sooner when the week of my arrival a *Mirror* crew was in a small plane crash while covering a desert train wreck. Their police reporter was killed. They had an opening for me.

Two months later, however, they made budget cuts and as the most recent hire I was laid off. City Editor Casey Shawhan said he wanted me back as soon as the cost-cutting wave passed and helped me get a PR job to tide me over.

I worked for a small agency, handling among other things the Pasadena Playhouse and what was called the Sixth Agricultural District Museum near the USC campus. The latter was a natural. I quickly changed the name to the Los Angeles Museum of Science and Industry and began generating a fair amount of publicity.

But I really didn't like PR work. That was another reason I hesitated when the Disney offer came and why I jumped at the first chance to return to the *Mirror*.

It was a fun newspaper to work at during those years, a wide open free-thinking tabloid. Witness my story about little David Potthast's pre-opening trip to Disneyland. I covered murder trials and John Wayne's divorce, the Lana Turner inquest in the death of Johnny Stompanato and Liz Taylor's marital shakeups. I even edited a zone section and wrote a daily column for a year. But, the *Mirror-News* (the "News" was added when we absorbed another paper) suddenly folded at the end of 1961.

I got a job as a feature writer with the *Long Beach Press-Telegram*, a job where I pretty much picked my own story ideas. I liked that, so when the chance to go to Disneyland came, it took several days to convince me to go back into PR. It proved the best move and the best job I could ever imagine, but I never realized in 1963 what amazing experiences lay ahead.

My first office was in the magnificent City Hall building on Main Street, U.S.A., but two years later, as seen in this photo, we moved to a temporary trailer just off Town Square with anything but an Imagineered Victorian styling.

Chapter 3

$\mathcal{B}$etween the 1955 opening and 1963, when I joined the Disneyland cast, I saw Walt at least once a year at the annual picnic staged for press and other guests to show off what was new for that year. Many times the picnic was held in the Holidayland just outside the berm that surrounds the park — a berm like those used to shut out the outside world at motion picture studios. The "land" was an open field with a tent designed for company picnics as a part of group sales efforts.

One year we stacked shaved ice fifteen feet high and decorated it with watermelons for dessert. It made a pretty centerpiece, but it took a week for the ice to melt, during which time Holidayland was too muddy to use. Disneyland frequently gave the press pink picnic baskets filled with fried chicken and other goodies. I still have one of the baskets.

Bringing large numbers of news people to our special events was a part of the basic publicity plan from the very beginning of Disneyland. It's a strategy that still continues for every major anniversary and new attraction at all the Disney parks — witness the recent year-long Disneyland fiftieth anniversary, celebrated in all the Disney parks. At Walt Disney World, upwards of fifteen thousand special guests were entertained for such major press events.

Before Disneyland opened, Eddie Meck went to Walt and told him, "You can't plant Disneyland like I used to do with movies. It's just too fantastic and different. They won't believe our stories."

"What are you going to do?" Walt asked.

"We'll get the press to come and see for themselves and the park will sell itself."

And that's why we created the press-invited opening, the annual picnics, the press passes for media and families, the trips we took to meet and tell the press what we were doing. Eddie taught me all of that.

For me, the biggest and best press "party" was held in 1959 with the grand opening for the first multi-million dollar additions — *The Matterhorn* with its racing bobsleds, the *Submarine Voyage* under the North Pole, the Disneyland Monorail system later extended to the Disneyland Hotel and a new *Autopia*.

Vice-President Nixon and his family dedicated the monorail. Meredith Willson conducted a five-hundred-piece band playing "Seventy-six Trombones" with seventy-six trombones in the lead. Willson's hit Broadway musical, *The Music Man*, from which the song was taken, had opened to rave reviews in 1957 and was still running. Skaters performed on an ice rink at the base of the *Matterhorn*, mountain climbers scaled to the top and giant toys marched in what was I always thought was the best parade ever.

A similar parade was staged during the Christmas season that year. A few years later, in a Disneyland souvenir book, the parade was pictured in a double-page spread showing the toy train passing through Town Square. In the middle of the parade, blocking the second float, is some crazy guy taking a picture with a big Speed Graphic Camera. I looked at it I three times before I realized *the photographer was me!*

I've always disliked *amusement parks*, but Disneyland, as Walt insisted, is not an "amusement park." I agree with a vengeance. Even on television people could see the park was entirely different from anything that had been done before.

It was designed with artistic attention to scale, design and color, with beautiful flowers and trees everywhere. Cast members, not employees, wore costumes, not uniforms, meticulously designed to fit in with their role and their surroundings. They were carefully trained to treat every visitor as a special guest. Music was added to complete the mood of each area.

Wherever you looked there was a unique view, with movement and color and what Walt called the "wienie" at the end of each exciting vista — down Main Street, the Castle; into Frontierland, the Riverboat or log cabins on Tom Sawyer Island; through the Castle in Fantasyland, a glimpse of galloping horses on *King Arthur's Carrousel*. It made you want to go see what was at the end of the road.

By the time I began work at Disneyland in 1963, the park was already the industry leader in many ways, including operations and maintenance. One of my first assignments was working with writer Kevin Wallace from the *New Yorker* magazine looking for Disney secrets of cleanliness and crowd control as it might relate to the then upcoming New York World's Fair.

We discovered them together, and I was as fascinated as the New York journalist. Based on Walt's experience taking his own daughters to Long Beach Pike and other amusement parks, he insisted on cleanliness above all. By the end of the first summer, however, the park was beginning to get a little worn looking. An outside janitorial contractor just wasn't able to clean up all the trash every night.

So before leaving to make a movie in Europe, Walt ordered his staff to get rid of the outsiders and "get this place clean." They soon discovered that the overnight cleanup wasn't working. So instead of cleaning entirely at night, they put two-thirds of their clean-up cast to work keeping things picked up during the day.

One of the first stories we heard was about the Main Street sweeper with his little broom and covered dustpan following a woman who was carrying a dirty paper cup. Finally, she got disgusted and said, "Young man, if you don't stop following me with that pan I'm going to throw my cup in it."

Keep it clean, they discovered, and it will stay clean. Let it collect all day and there will be a mountain of trash. Attractive themed trash cans were placed everywhere. I would see people walk clear across the street to put in their trash. And there were no signs pleading for them to discard trash properly. It was just part of the magic. Try that in Yankee Stadium.

And it had to stay new looking. Streets and buildings were washed down with a fire hose and brass was polished every night. Painters were constantly at work at night and on days when the park was closed, keeping it bright.

Because at ground level the store fronts along Main Street U.S.A. took a daily beating from guests — little nicks and scratches — while the upper level stayed in good shape for a couple of years at least, the painters had a set of colors for the lower half that matched the upper half after it had faded for a year.

Thousands of rim lights outlining the buildings along Main Street, U.S.A. were changed on a carefully planned schedule. Gasoline-powered vacuum cleaners were developed to clean streets even during the day. A squadron of them went down Main Street following every parade to pick up the paper cups and trash dropped by spectators where they stood to view the procession.

Walt had based the scale of Main Street on the five-eighths scale locomotives of the *Santa Fe & Disneyland Railroad,* so Main Street vehicles and shops were scaled to match. But, it was a graduated scale. Doors of five-eighths scale would have been okay for kids, but not tall enough for adults, so the ratio began at full scale on the lower level, gradually diminishing as it reached the upper floors giving an illusion of greater height, a forced-perspective trick copied from motion picture set building.

Trees in areas like Main Street were carefully chosen to fit the scale of the buildings. They had to be constantly trimmed and given slow-growth hormones to maintain that scale.

Disney crowd control techniques have been studied by many expositions and fairs. Before Disney, amusement parks generally sold separate tickets at each attraction. Seeking ways to avoid the mobs lined up for ticketing at each attraction, Walt's staff soon came up with a ticket book plan with attractions rated A (10 cents) to C (50 cents). They were sold along with general admission at the Main Gate in packages of eight or ten, with additional tickets available at booths within the park.

Later a "D" ticket (1956 and an "E" ticket (1959) were added to the mix. From then on, the term was applied all over the country as a synonym for the best of anything. We knew it had really entered the vernacular when astronaut Sally Ride said of her first Space Shuttle trip, "This is definitely an E ticket!"

The Enchanted Tiki Room, still in the design phase, was the first new attraction I saw when I went to work early in 1963. There was a full-scale mockup on one of the studio sound stages in Burbank. The birds sang, the tiki gods beat on drums, and it was all run from a tape recorder. I had never seen anything like it.

The *Tiki Room* was Walt's first show using Audio-Animatronics. Sound and motion, using hydraulic and pneumatic "muscles" to create movement in hundreds of figures from birds to animals, were all coordinated by a single two-inch tape recorder, which Walt discovered by visiting Wernher von Braun's space laboratories. The controls were all located in a small room beneath the attraction.

As its opening neared, I witnessed Walt's amazing ability to oversee every little detail. Surveying the waiting area in front of the thatched-roof theater in keeping with Adventureland nearby, he noted the public would have to stand in the hot sun for at least fifteen minutes until the next show and quickly devised a solution — strips of colorful silk overhead to diffuse the sun.

When it opened, *The Enchanted Tiki Room* was not a part of the standard ticket book, Disneyland tour guides were told to remind guests at the end of their tour to go to the *Tiki Room* before leaving the park.

"No thanks, we don't need to," replied one guest. "We have one on the bus."

The Audio-Animatronics system soon became a mainstay for scores of other Disneyland attractions and in four attractions developed by Walt for the New York World's Fair. The Fair also produced what may have been the most embarrassing moment in Walt's life.

The Fair's president, Robert Moses, asked to see what kind of shows Walt could develop for the new exposition. He was the first outsider to be shown Disney's newest experiment, the Audio-Animatronics figure of Abraham Lincoln delivering a speech. The figure was unbelievably real as it stood up to deliver an inspiring address. Moses immediately declared he simply must have "Lincoln" for the Fair. Although it was still in an experimental stage, Disney reluctantly agreed to develop the figure as an attraction for the State of Illinois pavilion.

After several more months of testing, the innovative system was working fine in California. But it was a different story when it was moved to the fair grounds in Flushing Meadows near Shea Stadium in New York.

Walt prepared to unveil the amazing attraction to an invited group of press and VIP guests, including former governor and then UN Ambassador Adlai Stevenson. Illinois newsmen whose papers had been highly critical of spending state money on such a project were also invited. Walt was absolutely sure it would be a big hit, which it was later.

One big problem stood in the way. The figure worked well while Imagineers were programming it at night, but when it was turned on during the day would go though all kinds of un-programmed wild motions. Some called it spastic. Occasionally, it would suddenly "wake up" and scare the janitorial staff right out of their broomsticks.

It was still not working on the morning of Walt's press conference. He had to apologize and turn away a very disappointed group of VIPs. Walt was thoroughly embarrassed for perhaps the only time in his life. It took two more weeks for engineers to discover the problem. At night Shea Stadium's lights were on, reducing electrical voltage by a barely noticeable degree. During the day, full voltage threw the delicate electronic programming all out of whack.

Great Moments with Mr. Lincoln and three other Disney shows using Audio-Animatronics were among the top ten attractions at the Fair. They included GE's *Carousel of Progress*, Ford's *Magic Skyway*, with giant dinosaurs brought to life electronically, and a salute to the children of the world in *It's a Small World*, where hundreds of dancing dolls were shown in the folk costumes of many lands. All were later moved to become successful attractions at Disneyland and other Disney parks.

The Fair proved to Walt that Disneyland-style entertainment would be just as popular in the East as it was in California — paving the way for his decision to build a park on the East Coast.

He also proved that California didn't have a corner on the market for smiling young people to help run his park.

"You can't find those kind of people in our tough town," people in New York had told Walt, "especially for temporary jobs."

Again Disney proved the locals wrong. He went to Hunter College and other New York schools and hired a cast that could learn to smile the Disney way just as well and as fast as the Californians had.

For the *Carousel of Progress*, Walt built a scale model of a futuristic city with a skyscraper convention hotel at its center, ringed by giant circles with roadways radiating through residential areas. It was a first attempt at visualizing his plan for EPCOT — an acronym for Experimental Prototype Community of Tomorrow — which was kept secret for another two years after the Fair.

At the time, Walt told Imagineer Martin "Marty" Sklar it wasn't really what he had in mind but it would be exciting for people to imagine such a future city. Marty was perhaps closer to Walt than anyone when it came to conceptualizing future projects. In recent years, Marty has been the creative head of Walt Disney Imagineering — Disney's dreamer-in-chief.

Originally he had my job at Disneyland as a publicity writer. Marty, then editor of the *Daily Bruin* student newspaper at UCLA, was hired in the summer of 1955 to produce the *Disneyland News*, a newspaper with an 1890s theme, as a souvenir and information source for guests. After graduation the following year, he returned to become Eddie Meck's writer. Walt soon began calling on Marty to help with speeches and development of concepts for new attractions.

The day I moved into my office in the Police Station in 1963, Marty moved his to an office at WED Enterprises in Glendale (later re-named Walt Disney Imagineering) where Walt housed his Disneyland designers, pulled from their "day jobs" as animators, set designers, artists, lighting experts, engineers, machinists and all the other needed crafts. In 2006, Sklar was the last of the original Disneyland employees still working full time for the company.

WED was a fascinating place, Soon after my arrival, it moved into larger quarters in a giant warehouse once the distribution center for a perfume company. Here, eye-popping special effects were demonstrated before incorporation in Disney adventures. It was big enough to build full-scale mockups of scenes for new adventures. Thirty-foot dinosaurs were sculpted in clay, then cast as plastic skins and articulated with electronically controlled hydraulic and pneumatic muscles. The same method was used for all kinds of animal and human figures.

Each project began with a concept, then a storyboard, like Walt's way of making motion pictures, then sketches and drawings, and then detailed small-scale models from which engineering drawings were made. In many cases, the Imagineers created full-scale mock-ups of the projects. The scale models of every thing from castles to mountains were frequently taken to the park to help guide builders during construction of the attractions.

❧

When I first visited WED, Wathel Rogers, one of the original Imagineers, was laced up in a weird looking rig with straps on his head, arms and legs, almost like a man in the electric chair, but this one was hooked up to electronics. Wathel began as an animator at the Disney Studios before Walt asked him to apply his expertise in animation to the infant world of electronic programming. Wathel was going through the motions of "father" in the *Carousel of Progress*, which told the story of electricity in a series of homey scenes and was then being developed for the World's Fair.

Wathel's movements were recorded on a two-inch tape recorder then played into the Audio-Animatronics figure's controls, replicating Wathel's original movements. The programming was done at twenty-four frames per second just like motion pictures.

The two-inch tape recorder was the same one that Wernher von Braun introduced Walt to when Disney visited his Alabama space laboratories. Walt obviously learned other lessons there, because secrecy at Disney Imagineering was just as tight as it was at von Braun's rocket labs.

While I was there, Walt was watching Wathel's performance, suggesting changes and nodding approval. All I could do was stand in awe.

The mammoth "sculptures" in the dinosaur shows were programmed in much the same way, although the triceratops movements were created with switches and levers since there was a shortage of live models.

Later, programming was all done from a desk-size control board covered with buttons and dials to control each tiny movement of the figure during recording on computer discs. When computers became available, the major positions were set, then the computer would take over the tedious task of creating a smooth motion between, say, frame 2,005 and 4,010. Here was a technique that set Disney parks apart for generations.

❦

The happiest of the Audio-Animatronics shows, with hundreds of dancing doll-like figures in the costumes of many nations, was called *It's a Small World*. Recently some too-cute thinker decided to change the name to lower-case letters. Now the name appears as *"it's a small world."* But I always knew it as *It's a Small World*. I'll stick with that.

For the Fair it was definitely a hurry-up project. Pepsi-Cola arranged for Walt to build the adventure as a salute to UNICEF and the children of the world, but the contracts were not signed until a few short months before opening. (By the way, one of Michael Eisner's first corporate moves was to shift our offices in New York from Madison Avenue to the Pepsi-Cola building, where Pepsi board member Joan Crawford had her office in earlier days.)

With just a concept in mind, one of Walt's most talented artists, Mary Blair, took on the *Small World* project and produced a charming and very popular show at the Fair.

A whole new ride system was used, repeated in many later shows, in which flat-bottom boats are pushed along a flume by the force of water from pumps all along the way. That was one reason *Pirates of the Caribbean* could be changed from a walk-through to a float-through.

It's a Small World, with its hundreds of dancing dolls, was the first Audio-Animatronics show to deal with large numbers of figures, all singing the same song. The Sherman Brothers wrote the title song, one of those that sticks in your head for weeks after you ride through the show. I would hear whole groups of people singing it as they walked through the park hours after hearing it once, for the first time.

Dick Sherman told me what a thrill it was for him and his brother to go to Walt's office and play their latest songs for him.

"He always asked us to play "Feed the Birds" from *Mary Poppins*."

Like so many talented artists in every field, they did their best work when Walt was looking over their shoulders.

At WED were two large secret rooms — off limits to all but a very few, which didn't include me. I used to wonder about it when I was there researching stories on *Pirates of the Caribbean* in 1963. Three years later, I was able to see the other side of those walls, which were covered with giant aerial maps and drawings for the greatest adventure of Walt's entire career.

It's the one he talked to brother Roy about in the final days before his death, using ceiling tile squares as grids to outline what his project would encompass. It was a project Roy promised to see opened successfully in his own lifetime. It had no name then. Now we know it as Walt Disney World. Actually, there was a debate over the name after Walt's death. Disneyland East? Disneyland Florida? Or just Disney World?

It was Roy, I think, who it insisted it was to be *Walt* Disney World.

Frontierland under construction in 1955. Building a Disney park takes time, but sometimes a young boy's dreams can't wait. David Potthast posed a la Tom Sawyer, fishing in a dry river, for my first Disney feature story.

Chapter 4

$\mathcal{W}$alt wanted attractions for the whole family, not some attractions for adults and some for kids. As a family park, he insisted on no liquor in the Magic Kingdom. He certainly wasn't anti-alcohol. I used to see him at the end of a walk-through invite his staff up for a drink in his apartment above the Town Square Fire Department station. He was still raring to go although I thought many of his staff were too tired to enjoy their cocktails. For guests, there was a convenient bar at the Disneyland Hotel but none in the park. Disney hotels and parks built after Walt's death, like Epcot, incorporated cocktail lounges in dining locations but they were always low key.

Disney wanted a place where the whole family could have fun together, not just ad watching while the kids had fun. He didn't want Dad to have an excuse to say, "You guys go ride the rides while I visit the bar." The absence of liquor also cut down on fights and other nuisances frequently associated with amusement parks of the time.

Disneyland's success — even more than the imagination and attention to detail in its attractions — may be its people, what Walt called his cast. As did others, I soon learned when I started to work more than forty years ago that we were not employees but *cast members* — playing parts as hosts and entertainers on a vast outdoor stage. The people who come here are not customers but *guests*.

Our cast wears *costumes* not *uniforms*. For many years, salaried people wore coats and ties when "on stage." They are taught to be genuinely friendly to everyone regardless of age, race or personality. When asked directions they talk and point — no bad manners in that.

Working with personnel advisor and friend Van France, Walt developed a show-business-style educational program, using long-time Disney cast members as instructors, to teach the history and philosophy of Disney first — before training new hires for any particular role in the show. Showing Disney films gives cast members and their families a new appreciation for the product — Disney entertainment.

Along with all the other "executives," Walt habitually stooped to pick up litter wherever he saw it in the park. All of us did. Whenever he came into the park, every cast member knew, somehow, that "Walt is here!" It was like someone had turned on an electric energy machine.

In the early days, he spent nearly every weekend wandering through the park talking to guests to see what they liked and didn't like. Later, as his celebrity increased, that became nearly impossible because he was being stopped every few seconds for a picture or an autograph.

One day our photographer, Charlie Nichols, who had a moustache like Walt's, was up on a fourteen-foot ladder with a big view camera when a lady pulled at his cuff.

"Are you Walt Disney?"

"I just laughed," Charlie told me, "but I felt like saying, 'Sure lady, Walt is always up on fourteen-foot ladders taking pictures,' but I didn't say it."

Actually ladders of any size were not allowed on Main Street during operating hours because they could spook the horses pulling the streetcars. Walt never wanted maintenance work to be seen by guests. That was easier in the early days, when Disneyland was closed on Mondays and Tuesdays. We never have closed at Walt Disney World, so there are times during lighter attendance days when painters and carpenters can be seen at work during operating hours. I loved being there at midnight with no one around but maybe a soundman checking amplifiers both inside and out.

Walt didn't like pictures of the park taken when no one was there. It needs people, he said. So we tried to shoot pictures with people having fun.

Much of Disneyland's inspiration came directly from Walt's childhood in Marceline, Missouri, including a life-long love of trains. The *Santa Fe & Disneyland Railroad* was a dominant attraction on opening day and remains a mainstay.

As a matter of fact, that train may have had more to do with Walt building Disneyland than any other factor. From the time he was a "candy butcher," or vendor, on the railroad between Kansas City and his home in Marceline, Walt never lost his love for choo choos.

During the 1930s, when overwork began to threaten Walt's health, doctors advised him to get a hobby as a way to let off steam. He turned to the studio's mechanical shop, which maintained motion picture cameras and other film gear.

With the help of two technicians in his machine shop, Roger Broggie and Earl Vilmer, Walt built a scale model steam locomotive he named for his wife, the *Lilly Belle*. Later he built railroad cars and had a small track laid around his Holmby Hills estate on Carolwood Drive. He called it the Carolwood-Pacific Railroad and would invite friends and their children to come out and ride the train, which was barely big enough for Walt to sit on as engineer.

In fact, trains played an important part many times in Walt's life. It was on a train returning from New York in 1928 and trying to replace the purloined cartoon series, *Oswald the Lucky Rabbit*, that Walt came up with the idea for Mickey Mouse.

During the final weeks before Disneyland's opening, Walt would invite friends including L.A. newspaper publishers to come down and ride his train in Disneyland. Walt's enthusiasm spilled over as he played engineer, which may explain the advance interest in the park among area newspapers and why all of them covered the press premiere with multiple reporters.

Disney personally invited one of his favorite animators, Ward Kimball, to bring his Firehouse Five Plus Two Dixieland Band to play for the Disneyland opening. Sharing Walt's life-long love of trains, Ward chose to play atop the *Santa Fe & Disneyland* freight train as it chugged its way around the park. Ward formed the band of Disney artists and animators as a lunchtime hobby. During World War II, Kimball's jazz group had toured local military camps in USO shows and begun making records while still keeping their day jobs.

Later the Dixieland group played nightly during the summertime at Disneyland, usually at the Golden Horseshoe Saloon in Frontierland. I used to come to the park after work just to watch their hijinks.

It was Ward who told me years later how he and Walt had gone to Chicago for the 1948 Chicago Railroad Fair to see an exhibition of new and old trains from steam locomotives to the first streamliners, Burlington Zephyr trains. Because of who he was, Walt was allowed to go down to the Fair for several mornings before opening and drive the trains.

"We had a ball," Ward recalled. Kimball had a large collection of HO and O gauge trains in his Glendale garage.

So I really think the inspiration for Disneyland was to satisfy Walt's desire for a bigger train to drive.

Walt's favorite pastime in the first years was sitting on the banks of the Rivers of America in Frontierland, looking across to Tom Sawyer Island as log rafts carried guests to the adventures inspired by another famous Missourian, Mark Twain. Not finished in time for the 1955 opening, it was completed a year later.

Taking famous stories and bringing them to life in movies or in Disneyland attractions was a staple of the Disney success. In the case of Tom Sawyer Island, Walt added a human touch by hiring a live Tom Sawyer in the person of thirteen-year-old Tom Nabbe. Stationed on the island's dock, Tom would help young "fishermen" bait their hooks as they pretended to be Tom and Huck's pals.

Nabbe was a red-haired, freckled-face spittin' image of Mark Twain's hero. He had sold newspapers outside the Disneyland gate during the first year. That gave him a chance to "pester" Walt for a job and when the island opened, Walt finally gave in, arranging Tom's work schedule around his school hours until he finished high school.

Tom always made a good feature story talking about how he met Walt. Except for a stint in the army, Tom remained a Disney cast member for more than forty-five years, working in operations at Disneyland and Walt Disney World, going to Disneyland Paris for two years to run its warehouses and then returning to manage even larger warehouses in Florida until his retirement, still a "young man" with freckles. He was added to the list of Disney Legends in 2005.

Tom received another honor reserved for those who have made a special contribution to the design or operation of Disney parks. His name was added to the signage on the windows of the "offices" above the shops that line Main Street, U.S.A. I saw that upstairs window on Main Street at Walt Disney World the other day. "Sawyer's Fence Painting Co.," it says, "Tom Nabbe, proprietor." Nice!

The Rivers of America was the setting for two of my favorite events during my seven years at the California park.

The first was in 1964 when Los Angeles hosted the U.S. Olympic team on its way to Japan. Walt was co-chairman of the host committee. The whole team came to visit Disneyland for a day. The hundred-yard-dash champions were the slowest walking people I ever followed around the park.

That night, Walt and his Hollywood friends put on a show for the athletes on a riverfront stage in Frontierland. Bob Hope was on stage doing his stand-up routine. Walt was in the front row. Suddenly the shrill toot of the little train in *Nature's Wonderland* cut loose.

Without missing a beat, Bob quipped, "Walt, your waffles are ready."

Another stage was erected on the tip of Tom Sawyer Island for the annual fall production of *Dixieland at Disneyland*. We had bands like Louis Armstrong, Pete Fountain, Kid Ory, and other legends coming to play at locations all around the park. For a kick-off to the evening in its first years we had tailgate parades with musicians loaded on wagons on Main Street, but then for several years added a great pageant on the Rivers of America.

Mounting the stage on the tip of Tom Sawyer Island was Ben Pollack's Jazz Band or Turk Murphy's San Francisco group. Others like the Dukes of Dixieland or Sweet Emma would float into view aboard Huck Finn Rafts, Mike Fink Keel Boats and Indian War Canoes.

The finale came when the *Mark Twain* hove into view with a cast of hundreds waving sparklers, a two-hundred-voice choir massed on the main deck. Above, on the Texas Deck, Louis Armstrong was trumpeting "When the Saints Go Marching In." It never failed to bring the crowd in the bleachers along the riverbank to their feet and elicit a deafening cheer from everyone in the area.

Entertainment Director Tommy Walker mused, "Some day we will do this show with actors playing the roles of those legends up there."

It was Walt who added the running gag that stopped the show one year. A musical trio aboard an Indian War Canoe came past at least three different times playing a slap base, guitar and clarinet. On their last appearance the bass player got so slap happy he turned over the canoe, the crowd screamed and the players swam back to shore dragging their instruments. Definitely a Disney touch.

Another typically Disney gag came in the first big Christmas parade in 1959 when a man carrying a cluster of giant red, blue and pink balloons handed the strings to a small boy who promptly rose into the air to the gasps and screams of those below. Until they realized the "boy" was just a dummy.

Walt never got to enjoy what surely would have been his favorite gag place in Club 33, a members-only dining area for company representatives from the sponsored attractions in the park. In the club he built a second, private dining room equipped with microphones in the chandeliers so that backstage performers could eavesdrop on dinner table conversations. Then, through speakers in the stuffed moose, elk and other taxidermy specimens hanging on the walls, the animals could talk with Walt's dinner guests. It was never finished, but the rest of Club 33 remains a semi-secret dining getaway for its members.

Massive balloon releases and the flight of carrier pigeons representing doves of peace were featured in Disney events at all the parks for years until it was discovered that balloons could possibly endanger sea turtles if they landed on Florida beaches. Pigeons were also released each night at sunset during flag lowering "retreat" ceremonies in Town Square. At Walt Disney World the release had to be curtailed when hawks in the neighborhood began harassing the pigeons heading for home in coops behind Cinderella Castle.

Walt always said, however, "If you have balloons and pigeons, you have a show." They were a big part of Walt's annual press picnics and grand openings, such as the one for *Nature's Wonderland* in 1960.

The *Nature's Wonderland* opening was a special time for me and other reporters who covered the event. At the end of the day, I was in a group of news people who asked Walt to tell us about his next big project. He talked for an hour. He never wanted to talk about past projects but always the next big adventure.

"Well," he said, "It's called *Pirates of the Caribbean* and we'll have scenes of pirates raiding the Spanish Main, pillaging treasure caves and burning the town."

He described it in such vivid detail we could actually see the flames. It was the most exciting story I had ever heard. Forty-five years later it became the basis of a smash-hit movie.

Just listening to him talk was an adventure in itself.

To me Walt's greatest genius was his ability to transmit excitement. It wasn't just his words that created the picture in other people's minds. Somehow he conveyed his vision for a movie scene, a visual story gag, a new character, a whole Disneyland adventure, even the concepts for a song, so that his creative team could see in their own minds what he was seeing. It was almost mystic.

A prime example is the story Herb Ryman told us during a lunch meeting years later. Walt phoned him one Thursday in 1954 and said he needed help laying out a map of Disneyland. Herb had done many artistic jobs for Walt and was living in Palm Springs at the time. He agreed to help.

But then Walt told him he needed to do it right away because Roy was leaving for New York on Monday and needed an illustration to show to the bankers he hoped to interest in the Disneyland project. Herb was dumbfounded and tried to back out, saying there was no way to finish over the weekend. Walt cajoled, finally promising he would stand over Herb's shoulders the entire time.

They began work on Friday. Absorbing Walt's ideas, Herb mapped a Fantasyland and Sleeping Beauty Castle, Frontierland with log fort and paddlewheel steamboat, a jungle in Adventureland, Victorian buildings on Main Street and a sleek modern Tomorrowland. The latter, being a little less clear in Walt's mind, was partly hidden by a giant hot air balloon floating overhead. Herb colored the areas in with green trees and muted colors.

The last I saw, that rendering was on display in the basement hallway between the two parts of the Disneyland admin building. You can look at today's aerial maps and see almost exactly the same thing except for the hot air balloon. Walt and Herb mapped out the look of Disneyland in three days. And not very much sleep, I guess.

Chapter 5

Walt had an unusual management style — far different from what has since become the vogue in MBA schools and many big corporations. His was sometimes called paternalistic. Certainly he made the decisions down to the last detail. Perhaps, now that the company has gotten so big, that kind of management would be impossible, even if Walt were here. But it was amazing — and great fun for me — to watch how it succeeded.

On those regular walk-throughs, Walt noticed every detail and made decisions quickly. One time he spotted a light in Tomorrowland pointed in the wrong direction and told someone to fix it. When it was still there two weeks later, well, the air was blue.

There's a legend that Howard Hughes once walked through a newly purchased aircraft plant. When he got through he said only, "Paint it."

If that had been Walt he would say, "Paint it a soft and pleasing color, use a lighter color on the ceiling and do it at night when it won't interfere with operations."

He held frequent but usually short meetings with his directors on each aspect of the company, usually an hour or so each. Disneyland, followed by a movie story conference, followed by screening of rushes, followed by merchandising, Imagineering, film distribution and maybe ending the day with the Sherman brothers coming into his office to play their latest song for *Mary Poppins*. Then he would take home scripts to read at night.

The meeting could end almost in mid-sentence at times. A week or a month might pass before a meeting on the same subject. Walt would resume the discussion right where it left off.

Out of those meetings came quick decisions, sound advice and a kind of inspiration you could see after his coworkers emerged from the meetings. They always seemed to come up with better ideas after a talk with Walt.

Never a backslapper, Walt didn't run around praising people for good work. He expected it. But one nod of approval or a smile from Walt was enough to keep his creative people enthused for days.

The boss didn't spend all his time in meetings. He would wander through the halls from one animator's little cubicle to the next, seeing what was going on, spotting special talents. Blaine Gibson was assigned as a sculptor at Imagineering after Walt spotted a tiny carved figure perched on his Movieola, the machine animators and editors used to run motion picture film on a small viewer. It was just a hobby model but it changed Blaine's career.

The Animation Building at the Studio, built in 1939 with the profits from *Snow White*, was was laid out somewhat like a hospital, leading to the legend that the banks financing the project demanded that it could be transformed into a hospital in case the studio failed.

In each of several wings leading from the main corridor there was a "nurse's station" at the entrance, which was sometimes used for a receptionist, and then individual rooms with connecting doors off each hallway. That's where the animators worked and a crazy bunch they were when I first toured their cubicles. They were really wonderful whackos.

There was Ward Kimball and Big Roy Williams, Frank Thomas and Ollie Johnston and other animators who were later were called "the nine old men." Ward told how they would open all the connecting doors, put a target at the end of the halls, holler for everyone to stand back and then pull out a bow and shoot arrows through the corridor they created.

One time, they say, following a tongue-in-cheek argument between two of the artists, one fired a blank shotgun shell, causing everyone in the building to come rushing out.

On the top floor of the building was a private lunchroom for the animators. Walt often ate there or in the Coral Room adjoining the employee cafeteria. That was always where he entertained our press groups for lunch. You could always see important stars, producers and directors lunching there. I remember the lunches I attended were very special, a chance to listen to Walt.

Walt's use of television to spread the word on Disneyland while getting paid to produce the show is only one of many examples of the *synergy* that has been a dominant factor in the company's success ever since the first Mickey Mouse toy was licensed seventy-five years ago. Motion pictures have always been the creative fountain from which this synergy flows, but the interactive benefits of all that Disney produces is nothing short of amazing.

People who see the movies buy the records, the videos, the plush toys and the Mickey Mouse watches. People who buy the watches and records are the ones most likely to visit Disney parks. Disneyland visitors are the ones most likely to go watch the Disney Channel and other Disney television shows, which in turn help to promote the parks and the movies.

For years, Mickey Mouse and Donald Duck comic books were among the biggest sellers in every country of the world. I remember finding a store called the Mickey Mouse Nut Shop with Mickey's image on its sign in Aswan near Egypt's biggest dam. Kids in Poland were carrying Mickey Mouse lunch boxes, although probably not ones properly licensed for sale there.

On my first trip to Mexico, our tour bus driver got lost. It was after dark. We wondered where we were and finally came to the small city of Leon. First thing I saw was a billboard atop the town's tallest building with a picture of Snow White and the Seven Dwarfs. "Visit Disneylandia," it said.

Until 1963, the year I started at Disneyland, Mickey Mouse watches were strictly for kids — $2.95 a shot. I had one of his pocket watches made by the first licensee, Ingersoll Watch Co., when I was seven years old, carried it in my hip pocket until I fell down and smashed it. Some things you remember.

By 1963, Ingersoll had become Timex, which made Mickey Mouse and other character wrist watches by the tens of thousands, inexpensive but good enough for kids. Disneyland merchandisers were hearing requests from adults for a "good" Mickey Mouse watch.

They approached Timex, which decided it wasn't worth the risk. They needed to sell several thousands to make it worthwhile, but were willing to let Disney approach other manufacturers.

Hamilton agreed to make one for around the unheard of price of $60. They produced one hundred and shipped them to Disneyland where they were sold out before they arrived, mainly to cast members. After the fifth shipment, I was able to buy one with its glass back for watching the wheels go round. It remained my prize watch until I moved to Florida and lost it picking tangerines with my son's Boy Scout Troop, one of life's tragedies because the original would probably be worth big bucks today.

Later Elgin and Seiko and even Baume and Mercier began making Mickey watches, which sold for hundreds of dollars. Collectors sell some of the old models for thousands. There are at least two fan clubs with thousands of members who spend weeks each year buying, selling and exchanging memorabilia.

Now, there must be a thousand variations of Mickey Mouse watches including a diamond-studded model at $15,000, plus watch faces for a hundred other characters. I must have at least twenty-five of them in my drawer.

When I wore the first one, it was enough to cause heads to turn in bars or restaurant. Now they are worn by everyone from kids in the ghettos to sophisticated millionaire bankers.

Disney works with cereal manufacturers, fast food restaurants, book publishers, magazines and many other major corporations on joint promotional programs with new and old Disney character toys, games and figures and Disney park trips as the prizes. Yeah, that helps sell more movie and park tickets. New films like *The Little Mermaid*, *The Lion King*, and *Aladdin* provide new characters, which then become major attractions in the parks or live shows utilizing music from the films.

Movies help drive business to Disneyland and the other parks. In return, the parks support the movies with signage, store window displays, in-room TV, and in scores of other ways. Sometimes, park entertainment division show directors help to produce extravaganzas for Disney movie premieres.

Merchandise always played an important part in Disney synergy from the earliest days when Mickey Mouse appeared on school lunch boxes.

In later years, movie cels, used to make animated motion pictures, became valuable collectors' items, selling for thousands of dollars. But when I first went to Disneyland in its opening year or two, they sold the cels for $1.75 each.

Jack Olsen, head of merchandise, who was one of my good friends after I started to work there, was at the Studio one day and saw a worker pushing a wheelbarrow full of cels.

"Where are you going with those?" Jack asked. They were out of room and had no place to store them. After all, there were twenty-four of those cels for each second on the screen. Jack told the wheelbarrow man he would take the cels, he thought he could make use of them. So he had them cut down and put in 5x7 frames and sold at Disneyland. (Cutting the cels actually decreased their value as collectibles, but then nobody anticipated cels like these selling for thousand of dollars.) I bought three of Donald Duck, Jiminy Cricket and Chip and Dale for my children's rooms when they were little.

Later I took them down, put them in a brown envelope and forgot all about it. When cels became collector's items, I remembered mine but couldn't find them. It was nearly forty years before I found them in the bottom of a bureau, had them framed and hung them in my den. I also have framed that blue ribbon from Disney-

land's Preview Day with my *Mirror-News* reporter business card attached. Nothing sentimental about me.

Main Street, U.S.A. takes shape at Disneyland. It was to be my workday destination for seven
years before I moved on to a similar Victorian boulevard in Florida.

Chapter 6

For Disneyland operations managers, safety was always the first consideration. While accidents do occur, the Disney safety record was always far better than most public places. Accidents were seldom a problem for our publicity department.

I always felt that because they were clean and well run, the parks promoted a friendlier feeling among guests for each other. We seldom see major arguments among guests. Frequently I would see veteran guests giving advice to newcomers about how to time their visits to save time waiting and have more fun.

Walt's focus was always on entertaining guests, spending his money on new and better adventures. Walt never wanted to build a big administration building.

"I can use that money for a whole new attraction," he would say.

Each year brought a major new attraction. He was finally talked into a three-story "admin" building but only because it could be built on both sides of the railroad track and encompass the new *Primeval World* display of dinosaurs brought back from the New York World's Fair in 1965. It was always inconvenient, though, because you had to go down to the basement and through a tunnel under the railroad tracks to get from one part of the building to another. Still, it was better than the overcrowded Dominguez bungalow with its lean-to storerooms that was still in use when I went to work at Disneyland in 1963.

～ら

One of the first times I had a chance to set up pictures of Walt in the park (except for new attraction openings) was early in 1964 when major additions were being made to the popular *Jungle Cruise*. He seldom had time to pose for us without a specific purpose in mind.

Walt was particularly proud of many new Audio-Animatronics animals in the jungle adventure that moved more realistically and looked more life-like than ever. He spent an entire morning inspecting the new animals, allowing photographer Charlie Nichols and I to go along and get several unusual candid shots of Walt on the job with several construction workers.

As always, Walt was more excited about something new, about to be completed, than something already finished. And he was always looking for ways to do it better.

Walt insisted the main thing in any attraction was the story.

"Disney doesn't build rides," he said. "Disneyland adventures tell stories and sometimes put you on cars, boats, trains or other vehicles, not for just riding but to carry you into and through an exciting story."

That's one reason he didn't want it called an amusement park where mostly you went to go on rides.

It was seven years after he first told our group of reporters about the new attraction before *Pirates of the Caribbean* became reality. Unfortunately it came four months after Walt's death. From that time forward *Pirates* has been my favorite attraction, but I'm not sure it was quite as fantastic as it seemed when Walt talked about it. Initial construction was postponed so that Disney Imagineers could build four major attractions for the New York Worlds Fair of 1964-65.

Steel beams for the *Pirates* adventure, which was to be built as part of a whole new area, New Orleans Square, were already in place when I arrived for work in 1963. The plan changed radically and grew during the next two years while the steel rusted. A water-flume boat system developed for *It's a Small World* at the Fair was incorporated into the revised plan for *Pirates*, so instead of a walk-through, it became a ride-through.

It was even more exciting that way because guests were always moving. Operationally it was better, too. Because guests moved at a steady pace, rather than having to wait for others to move on, it insured higher guest capacity. Construction started all over again in 1964.

The grand opening of *Pirates of the Caribbean* came in April of 1967 when we staged an attack by pirates sailing into Frontierland aboard the sailing ship *Columbia*, which is still a part of the Rivers of America fleet. With the Jolly Roger skull and cross-bones flying, they sailed with covering newsmen into the dock while high-jumping actor pirates leapt ashore with movie-style abandon. Television news cameras were on hand for filming, but without video tape it was a day later when it could be seen on television.

The attraction was actually ready to go on the original schedule in 1966 (in time for Walt to enjoy it during the opening of New Orleans Square) except for one thing. Boats going down that first water slide threw up a huge wave that engulfed the test engineers. It took them another six months to work out the bugs.

Walt did get to see all of the *Pirates* scenes and presided at the opening of New Orleans Square and the Blue Bayou Restaurant. The latter was closed after the opening day because Walt said it needed boats passing by to be complete.

Walt had fun with the mayor of New Orleans at the opening of New Orleans Square.

"It looks just like home," said the mayor.

"Only cleaner," replied Walt.

"Well, give it a hundred years," the Louisiana mayor retorted.

Fireworks were another of Walt's sure-fire crowd pleasers. In the second summer, in 1956, park officials were worried because no one stayed around after about six o'clock, although at Walt's insistence they remained open until nine.

"Close early," he was advised, "at least by seven. People are just too tired to stay after a long hot day."

"No," said Walt, showing his usual foresight, "We'll make nighttime so exciting, there will be a whole new crowd of guests who will come for the evening to hear music and watch the fireworks — every night, at least for the summer."

The Elliott Brothers Big Band became the star attraction. Visiting singers, dancers and bands including top names like Peggy Lee or the Benny Goodman Orchestra performed on various stages in each land. Not many came just to see those stars, but they would go back home telling friends, "I saw Peggy Lee at Disneyland!"

A local TV show, *Date Nite at Disneyland*, brought additional attention in those early years and giant fireworks bursting over Sleeping Beauty Castle became a tradition.

Neighbors in the area at first complained about the noise of the nightly fireworks, but soon began collecting on porches and rooftops to watch the show from afar. It made it hard to put the kids to sleep before nine, when the fireworks went off.

When *The Matterhorn* was built in 1959, Walt arranged to have Tinker Bell, in the person of an old time circus aerialist, slide down a wire flying over the castle to light the fireworks, just like the beginning of his TV show. She was a little old lady in her seventies at that time, less than five feet tall. She used the same kind of rigging she had used as a young circus performer. A different Tinker Bell flies every night at Disneyland and in the Magic Kingdom in the summer.

Eddie Meck told about a lady from Texas watching the pyrotechnics one night saying, "We have bigger fireworks in Texas!" Eddie said quietly, "Every night?"

Now every Disney park around the world features nightly fireworks much of the year. It must keep half the factories in China and Italy working overtime.

By 1957, Disneyland was *the* place where families, teenagers and young adults went for nighttime fun as well as during the day in the summer.

Dixieland music was a vital part of that entertainment on warm summer nights, not just at "Dixieland at Disneyland" in the fall. Walt invited Ward Kimball and his Band — with Ward on the broomstick slap bass and trombone — to play nights at the Golden Horseshoe Saloon for many years. Later Clara Ward and her Gospel singers took over that stage and Ward moved to New Orleans Square.

I remember the summertime picnic around 1958 when Walt first introduced the Young Men from New Orleans — all of them at least fifty-five years old — headed by seventy-year-old guitarist Johnny St. Cyr, who began playing on Mississippi steamboats more than fifty years before. The Young Men played on the deck of the *Mark Twain* as it made its way around the Rivers of America at night — pure nostalgia and more.

My daughter, Janet, at age seven would beg to go out to the park at night so she could dance up and down the stairs as the Dixieland band played. Bill Robinson never appeared, but she was Shirley Temple.

My friend Jack Smith in a *Los Angeles Times* column recounted a similar experience. He had met a youngster selling newspapers on the dock in a small village where Jack stopped while cruising up the west coast of Canada. He told the teenager "If you ever come to L.A., I'll take you to Disneyland."

When the teenager did manage to make the trip, Jack made good on his promise. After following him for a while Jack tired and let the youngster go ahead and have fun on his own. You always felt safe at Disneyland letting ten-year-olds and up go off on their own. As Walt planned it there was only one way out — up Main Street — so you could wait and meet them as they started to leave.

As Jack told the story in his column, he went for a quiet cruise up the river aboard the *Mark Twain*. As he stood watching the sun reflected in the muddy waters, he noticed a seven-year-old boy at the rail also staring off into the distance — perhaps lost in his own imagination.

"I don't know who he was," Jack wrote, "But I was Gaylord Ravenal." That year, *Showboat*, in which Howard Keel plays the dashing Ravenal, was revived for another successful run in movie theaters.

Sleeping Beauty Castle was to become a sort of unofficial logo for Disney parks around the world. This was the way it looked the first time I saw it in April, 1955. After fifty years is has become one of the most photographed structures in the world.

Chapter 7

$\mathcal{D}$isneyland became a place where celebrities came to be noticed. Liz Taylor and Eddie Fisher, who always loved publicity, made a "secret" visit to the park but were plainly not upset when wire service photographers turned up "accidentally."

We had instructions from Walt to treat the celebrities as ordinary guests and not exploit them for publicity purposes. I remember seeing Julie Andrews pushing a pram with her newborn baby soon after she became famous as Mary Poppins. No one noticed her. Several times political candidates came during national election campaigns. We always asked they not bring posters or wave signs but allowed them to go through on a handshaking tour as long as other guests were not bothered.

Nelson Rockefeller was the first presidential campaigner I saw, and I learned from his aides about leading a group of people through a crowd: Hold your hand high as a beacon for the candidate. Foreign tour operators hold up pennants or umbrellas at all the Disney parks to keep from losing their group in the crowds, but politicians like hands. George Wallace, Hubert Humphrey and Edmund Muskie all came to Walt Disney World on campaign tours during its early years.

Many of the visits were official tours sponsored by the State Department.

The U.S. delegation to the United Nations brought several tours of delegates to Disneyland, especially from developing nations. I remember one African delegate who, after riding the *Jungle Cruise*, observed a large crowd waiting to board the boats.

"I finally see how to make money out of Africa," he said.

Richard Nixon, who had been there many times including dedicating the monorail in 1959, opened his Presidential campaign in 1968 at Disneyland. I went with his tour on a warm summer evening as he rode the *Santa Fe & Disneyland Railroad* train with a few aides and made his way shaking hands through the crowd of curious guests. While still a reporter, I had covered Nixon's "farewell" after his defeat for the presidency in 1960. I was also there years later for his famous "I am not a crook" speech at Walt Disney World in 1974.

Bobby Kennedy's tour, also in the summer of 1968, was in direct contrast to the Nixon visit, a raucous affair as he and a large entourage shoved their way through midday crowds. A TV crew he had hired to chronicle the tour literally ran over people, including Bobby's own children, as they raced to try to get ahead of him, a microphone cord and soundman trailing the cameraman. Our security people finally had to ask the troupe to slow down and quit shoving people. They left shortly thereafter. Kennedy was assassinated a few nights later in Los Angeles.

Walt was very quiet about politics until later in life. He became interested when his friend George Murphy got into the U.S. Senate race. From then on Walt was openly a Republican supporter. He even wore his "Goldwater for President" button when he went to the White House to receive the Medal of Freedom from President Lyndon Johnson, who was not amused.

Among many other things, Walt was a true patriot. He showed it in his movies, in his life and certainly in his design of Disneyland and its entertainment. The American flag always flew in the parks. *Great Moments with Mr. Lincoln* is, I believe, Walt's proudest achievement. The even more impressive *Hall of Presidents* at Walt Disney World, completed years later, continues to add a new president each time one is elected, still following the plan Walt Disney created years ago.

No one can see those presentations, and the inspiring *American Adventure* performance at Epcot, without gaining a new appreciation for this nation and for Walt's vision.

In addition to steamboats and trains, Walt's love of animals was obvious. His first drawing as a child, according to legend, was the head of a horse belonging to a neighbor doctor in Missouri. Two years before Disneyland was to open, Walt hired Owen Pope and his wife, Dolly, to raise small horses to pull surreys up and down Main Street, U.S.A. Walt had seen Owen and his buckboard driving a team of little snow-white Shetland ponies at rodeo shows.

Owen started collecting and breeding the little ponies for the Disneyland job until he got his first look at the surreys. They were too big for the horses, so he had to start anew and collect a slightly larger horse troupe. I frequently visited Owen when I was writing feature stories for the *Long Beach Press-Telegram*. He always had a good animal story with pictures. He ran a pony farm on the north side of the Disneyland property, but the public never got to see it.

In pre-Disneyland days, one of Owen's charges was a little Sardinian donkey that Walt found when he traveled in Italy. Walt shipped him home, where he stayed on the studio back lot under Owen's care.

One of Walt's best friends in the Hollywood press corps was Lloyd Shearer, then entertainment editor of *Parade Magazine*. Lloyd came to interview Walt one day and brought his ten-year-old daughter so she could meet Walt. While the two men talked, Walt arranged to have the child taken on a tour of the back lot where she met the donkey.

The donkey promptly bit Lloyd's daughter on her hand, causing a minor wound. Studio aides quickly bandaged it and took the little girl back to Walt's office in tears. He was aghast.

"I don't understand," Walt told the child. "Usually he is the friendliest little fellow you ever saw. Come on, honey, let me show you."

So the three of them went out to the donkey's corral. Walt reached in to pet the donkey, who immediately nipped Walt's fingers. Sardinian donkeys, it seems, have a mean temper. That one disappeared right away.

Walt was forever finding things on his trips and sending them back home. One time Mrs. Disney waited impatiently in the car while Walt talked to a ranger at Petrified Forest. For her next birthday, her gift was a huge petrified stump Walt had purchased that day. She promptly donated it to Disneyland. I was there when it was placed by the river in Frontierland with a plaque acknowledging the "donation."

Owen Pope also collected a troupe of pack mules for Frontierland to carry guests on mule-back rides through *Nature's Wonderland.* For a couple of years, he kept horses to pull stagecoaches carrying guests through the same area.

One day Eddie Meck proved what good friends he had in the press. Two wire service photographers were walking through the park with Eddie when they all saw a horse drawn stagecoach overturned. Some guests were slightly injured.

One of the photogs turned quickly to Eddie and said, "What was that other picture spot you talked about in Tomorrowland?"

They left the accident scene without clicking a single shutter. I don't suppose that kind of reaction could happen today among the post Woodward and Bernstein press corps.

A few months later the stagecoach rides were eliminated. Surreys also had to be abandoned as the crowds on Main Street became heavier. But the draft horses and horse-drawn streetcars still remain.

Eddie Meck built his press friendships by treating photographers and reporters with fairness and by knowing what they needed. For the wire services at openings, he would arrange to set up a picture of Walt early in the day so they could meet their East Coast deadlines ahead of the planned ceremonies.

Another way we built and maintained press relations was by personal visits far and near. Instead of mailing our releases to the key Orange County and L.A. papers, we went down weekly to deliver information for the calendar-entertainment section and press releases about special events at the park. It gave us a chance to keep friendships alive. We never stayed long; we didn't want to become pests. Sometimes we took Disney characters to the city room at Christmas time, but only by prior approval.

One of my first contact trips outside the L.A. area was to Northern California. I stopped at the *Santa Cruz Sentinel*, where I only had a few minutes because of appointments in San Francisco. The editor turned out to be a fellow alumnus of the University of Missouri School of Journalism. That opened the door. We talked old school days and I told him about Walt's amazing new Audio-Animatronics system that could make birds, flowers and human figures come to life.

"I want you to talk to my humor columnist, I think he can get a story."

So with little time to spare I sat down at John's desk (I can't remember the last name) and mostly told him Disneyland anecdotes like the ones told in this book for his humor column. Toward the end I really hurried through and had to leave rather quickly to meet my other dates.

His column was all about this Audio-Animatronics press agent that Walt Disney had sent to talk with him.

"Toward the end of our conversation," his story said, "He seemed nervous and about to run out of talk. I realized afterwards he must have been low on battery power. If he had just said something I would have been glad to let him plug in to the outlet by my desk." So much for trying to keep myself out of the spotlight!

Making friends with newspeople wasn't always an easy job. Among the unusual annual events at Disneyland is an all-night party for graduating high school seniors, a tradition that still continues. It began with schools in the Anaheim area but within a few years began attracting seniors from far away.

The events were organized by senior classes and school officials. Because the park did not allow alcoholic beverages it was an
ideal place for underage youths. But kids being kids, some tried to
circumvent the rules. Some had tried such things as bringing in gin
strapped to their waists in hot water bottles with a plastic tube to
drink from. So we instituted a policy of searching all attendees for
contraband and our security people got very good at keeping the
events alcohol free.

When the first schools from the San Francisco area decided to
attend, we notified Bay Area papers. One paper sent a veteran reporter I will refer to simply as Joe Reporter to report on the high
schoolers' activities.

He arrived with the chaperones and students for the all-night
affair at about ten and was searched at the front gate along with
everyone else. Joe made no bones of the fact that he resented the
"invasion of privacy."

Right after arrival, he announced he was going to the Disneyland Hotel to meet his brother just returned from the South Pacific.
Four hours later, in the wee hours, I got a call from Security. Joe
had returned drunk as a skunk, and I don't mean Bambi's friend
Flower, and mad as heck because our "hosts" had stopped him. He
was threatening to expose these "Nazis" and their high-handed
methods. I went out to talk to him and after a few minutes got him
calmed down enough to come and have a cup of coffee.

Later he apologized and wrote a very favorable review of the
trip.

Seven years later, at the first Walt Disney World All-Nite Grad
Party, accompanying students from a Florida school was — you
guessed it! — the same Joe Reporter, now relocated to Florida, just
like me. Only this time he was accompanied by his wife. Very quiet
and friendly he was when I bumped into him by pure chance at the
Main Gate. The no-liquor policy was not a problem.

There were really very few journalists, drunk or otherwise, who ever caused me any problems. Many became good friends. I wrote only two letters complaining about unfavorable stories in the entire time. It didn't do any good.

Most writers just had a good time and enjoyed writing about it. There was one, early on, a British humor writer and critic for *Punch* magazine named Alan Whicker who also had a popular TV show. He arrived during our construction to shoot a feature story and we reluctantly agreed because having any sort of film crew on the property was a perfect excuse for construction workers to lay down their hammers and watch.

With some limitations and a guide to keep them from falling into construction holes, the crew managed to shoot a day's worth of footage. But they wanted more. I finally agreed to one more half day, but when they still wanted more, I came down hard. Whicker wrote later that, after all those smiling people who kept saying "Have a good day" during his visit, it was nice to meet a thoroughly nasty fellow like Ridgway.

I also chased a prominent freelance photographer off Main Street during the Grand Opening because he was standing right in front of our own TV cameras filming the opening special. He was shooting for *Time* magazine and threatened to blacken my name with them forever more, but I never heard anything later.

Working with photographers, as well as writers, was another big part of my job. I was continually amazed at their talents.

When I went to work at Disneyland, photographer Tom Nebbia was just wrapping up a six-month shoot for *National Geographic* on a complete story about Walt Disney, the first major profile on a single person ever in the magazine. My first job was to accompany the caption writer for two weeks while he assembled material to write the "legends" for the photos. The accompanying story had already been written well ahead. I was amazed at the meticulous detail and amount of time spent just on the captions.

Big-magazine freelance photographers were always a challenge to work with because they always wanted more and better angles. A prime example is photographer Larry Schiller. Larry was a real wheeler-dealer. He would sign up quadruplets to an exclusive five-year contract, selling their pictures to many magazines. Larry also had exclusive rights to execution photos of a convicted murderer in Utah who insisted on facing the firing squad. Schiller later became a producer of Tarzan movies among others.

But I knew him when he was just a photographer and came to do a feature on Walt and Disneyland for the *Saturday Evening Post*. He wanted high lifts and ladders, special lighting, characters with their heads off, pictures of the Audio-Animatronics figure of Mr. Lincoln. All were difficult if not impossible to accomplish, and we were able to meet most of his demands although some required Walt's personal approval.

The character picture became a shot of the heads of the Seven Dwarfs going across the parking lot in a pickup truck. His picture of Walt with Mickey Mouse, the White Rabbit, Pluto and Piper Pig crowded around became a classic. Larry gave me the original as a thank you and it wound up on the cover of Bob Thomas' biography of Walt Disney.

Many things changed at Disneyland in the seventies. Big bands and pop singers had been a regular part of nighttime entertainment through the sixties. We had a big band night every year with five or six big name swing bands plus the annual "Dixieland at Disneyland." We had groups like Benny Goodman, Artie Shaw, Xavier Cugat and the Osmond Brothers, whose debut with their barbershop quartet act was a hit. In the late sixties, hootenanny and folk music became big but although it was growing fast, we never had any rock 'n roll until the end of the decade, when the Bell Sisters came to perform one summer. I think they were only about twelve years old, young and innocent, but there was some consternation when they began singing rock and roll in what some called a haven of conservatism.

Up to then "hippies" and "long hairs" were not welcome. In fact, men with long hair were not admitted until a prominent Hollywood actor appeared one day. It took a call to Card Walker, Walt's Director of Marketing, to break the ban. The policy gradually changed after that.

Since he viewed Disneyland as a family entertainment place, Walt insisted on a code of dress for both cast members and guests. Cast members were not permitted facial hair, long hair, bright nail polish and so forth. For guests, prohibitions in the park included bathing suits, short shorts, shirtless men, see-through blouses for women, bare feet or any gang jackets or group attire that was likely to cause conflicts with other logo-clad groups. Safe and well-behaved was the order of the day.

As I say, the world changed and Disney changed with it without abandoning altogether a family entertainment concept.

I only recall one time when Walt's temper flared — and it was at me. We were taking pictures of the opening of the *Columbia* sailing ship below decks. Fowler had arranged for a navy admiral to be on hand for the ceremonies. Walt was taking him around the deck and below, pointing out all the incredible little details. It was taking forever. The press photographers were pushing me to hurry along for their deadlines.

"We would like you over there by the rail, Walt," I said.

"We'll be there when I get ready," he said with fire in his eye.

Somehow I decided to back off. Walt was known for losing his temper at times. Bob Thomas' biography tells of several such occasions, even with Roy or other close associates. But he never seemed to remember or hold a grudge. If the incident came up he would frequently just laugh about it.

But when Walt called, his top people came in a hurry. I remember Card Walker, who was very close to Walt and his chief adviser on marketing, would literally run from his office if the phone rang from Walt's office. Card, who became President and then Chairman of the Board after brother Roy's death, was himself an inspiration to me and always kind even if I blundered. I always knew I could call Card directly if I had a question.

I remember early on sitting in the bleachers in Town Square watching a Disneyland parade with several of my newspapers friends. We were having a good time. I remember overhearing Card sitting behind us tell Eddie Meck with a note of surprise in his voice, "They really like Charlie."

That may have carried me through a lot of Disney years.

Flying in Walt's plane — which bore the call letters 234MM (for Mickey Mouse) — was great fun, although flying from coast to coast at prop jet speeds was a pretty long trip. Chuck Malone and the other pilots, all of whom knew Walt intimately because of their long hours together, were always accommodating and friendly to other passengers.

My first long trip aboard "the Mouse" was from Los Angeles to New York. Gretta and I were taken with other Disneyland managers to see the New York World's Fair. The flight required a refueling stop, frequently at Grand Island Nebraska. (They gave green stamps which just about furnished Chuck's house for him.) Airport operators would roll out a red carpet and bring out a tin of fresh baked cookies each time we stopped.

Later we flew into Orlando several times during construction of Walt Disney World. We always landed at Herndon Field instead of McCoy (later Orlando International) where they regularly announced, "Mickey Mouse 234 approaching." Then, after landing, it was, "The Rat is on the ramp."

We were landing in Phoenix one night on a personal appearance trip with Disney characters. The main airport was closed for runway paving. We were approaching the substitute, a Navy air station. The tower advised, "There's a Navy jet coming in behind you but if you hurry on in you can beat him." Chuck turned the plane on its nose, left my stomach at nineteen thousand feet and screeched to a perfect landing.

After he died, I used to sit in Walt's seat near the rear of the plane, remembering. This was his third plane. He loved flying almost as much as train travel, maybe more by then. He bought a Queen Air, then a King Air, mainly for weekend trips to his home in Palm Springs. The Mouse, for cross-country trips, was a Grumman Gulf Stream prop jet.

The plane was known by nearly every air-controller across the country. All of them seemed to have a warmer note in their voices when they said the words *Mickey Mouse*. I think the plane is still sitting at the Disney-MGM Studios in Florida where it was brought in retirement so park guests could see it. And now, when you see it, you know the rest of the story.

One of the best parts of scoping out Orlando was that Gretta and I got to fly there on Walt's private plane, MM234, affectionately known by air traffic controllers as "The Mouse." Local airport staff loved to announce, "The rat is on the ramp."

Chapter 8

I guess I have to take the blame for letting the monster out of the bag prematurely when the "Florida project" was first discovered by the rest of the world. It didn't even have a name at the time.

It was in the fall of 1965. Disneyland had been celebrating its tenth anniversary, an event we called the *Tencennial*. For a year, we had been using Walt's plane to fly in travel writers from various parts of the country.

When the World's Fair projects were completed, Walt's plane stayed busy. He arranged for cast members like me to fly East with our wives to see what Disney had done for the Fair. And he told Eddie Meck to use the plane to bring press to Disneyland for the *Tencennial*.

The plane held fourteen passengers, so our press trips would bring a half-dozen writers and their wives for a weekend visit to the park and its new attractions. During the first nine months of 1965, we had already flown travel writers from the Midwest, the East and West Coast but were told to hold off on the South because "papers there were all focused on civil rights marches."

One of the groups that year stands out in my mind, the one when travel editors John Hughes of the *New York Daily News* and John McCloud of the *Washington (DC) Daily News* came to see our *Tencennial*. Toward the end of a busy day and still suffering from jet lag, the two Johns were resting on a bench just outside the Golden Horseshoe Saloon while their wives went shopping.

Three women suddenly stopped in front of the two dozing writers. "Don't they look real," said one woman to her companions, obviously used to seeing Audio-Animatronics figures that were just as life-like. Hughes and McCloud didn't bother to move.

Finally, toward the end of our Tencennial we decided to bring in a group from the South. We invited writers from Miami, Fort Lauderdale, Atlanta and Birmingham. The *Miami Herald* and *Atlanta Constitution* declined the invitation.

The *Miami News* sent feature writer Howard Kleinberg, who later became editor of the paper and a columnist for Cox Newspapers. The executive editor of the *Fort Lauderdale News Sentinel* agreed to come. Writers from the *Birmingham News and Post-Herald* were on board. We needed two more to fill the plane.

Someone said, "What about Orlando?"

"What's Orlando?" I replied, showing off my geographical ignorance.

We looked it up. It had a good-sized paper, the *Orlando Sentinel*, so we called the managing editor, who agreed to send his Sunday Editor, Emily Bavar. We also invited the Ocala, Florida-based editor of a Sunday magazine that appeared in several Florida weekly papers.

The night before the plane was due, I got a call from some guy at the Disney Studios I had never heard of before (or since) who said, "What's this I hear about you bringing in some press from Florida?"

"Yeah," I said, "We've been bringing in press for the Tencennial for nearly a year."

"Well, you know you can't tell them anything about the Florida Project," he warned.

"What Florida project?" I replied.

"Well, I guess if you don't know anything, you can't very well tell them."

"But they are having lunch with Walt tomorrow," I advised.

"That's Walt's problem."

Sure enough, the minute Emily got off the plane in California she began asking about rumors that Walt was buying a large tract of land near Orlando.

"Beats me," I said. "He has always said there would never be another Disneyland because he wanted to be near enough for him to oversee in person. You'll have to ask him tomorrow."

So, the next morning they met Walt before lunch. Emily asked about the rumor.

Walt, she said later, had given them a long song and dance about having looked at land in that area but decided against it because . . . and he then quoted a lot of vague and outdated statistics.

"Walt was not a good liar," Emily said frequently.

The group went to lunch where I joined them. Those press lunches were where I really got to know Walt's personality. He was always at his best with the press. We posed the group for pictures. Walt, as usual, stood on tiptoes so he would look a little taller in comparison to tall people like the Fort Lauderdale editor, Fred Pettijohn. The photos were sent as souvenirs to the group. Emily showed me hers twenty-five years later.

Without saying anything to the others, Emily and the editor from Ocala went back to the Disneyland Hotel and sent stories by teletype. The Ocala writer's wire editor promptly lost the story. It didn't seem very important, I guess.

Emily Bavar's story arrived late at night. They used it the next morning with a one-column headline way down at the bottom of page one.

"Rumor Disney Buying Land."

No one paid very much attention, because all kinds of big names had been rumored to be the buyers — Howard Hughes, Ford Motor Company and other space-related industries. Martin-Marietta was at the time the big company in town, doing space work.

State officials, who necessarily had been in on the secret, gave it the code name *Pluto*. Those who heard it assumed the name related to the space program like *Saturn* or *Apollo*, not a "cartoon" movie star.

Emily returned home Monday. When she got to the office Tuesday morning she was quizzed at length about her basis for thinking Disney was the buyer. Her editors decided she was right.

On Thursday morning a huge banner headline — **"We Say It's Disney"** — labeled the rumor as true. The story gave my newspaperman's sense of humor a jolt. It said in effect, "We're sorry folks, we underplayed the story on Sunday, so here it is again and you can believe it this time."

For the *Tencennial*, we had prepared a huge kit of stories and pictures about Disneyland, its history and detailed descriptions of all of its attractions. During the following three weeks the *Sentinel* ran every scrap of information we had supplied, to show what could be coming to Central Florida, and asked for more.

Other state newspapers jumped into the fray. Wire service reporters badgered Florida Governor Hayden Burns until he was forced to confirm the rumor and announced there would be a press conference in Orlando a month later to unveil details.

The announcement sessions in November, one for state and local community leaders and one for the press, were held in the Egyptian Room at the Cherry Plaza Hotel on Lake Eola. Walt, Roy and Governor Burns sat at the head table. It was reported this was the largest press conference ever held in Florida, including President Franklin D. Roosevelt's vacation trips and those during space shots at Cape Kennedy. Among the guests was a young legislator from Lakeland, Lawton Chiles, who later became governor and helped us reenact the event for its twenty-fifth anniversary.

Radio, TV and newspaper people from the entire state came. The *Sentinel* ran a picture on page two of one of its photographers literally hanging from the chandelier to get a shot of the head table which ran on page one.

Actually, the *Sentinel* had a full rundown of what was to be announced in its morning edition before the conference. I asked Bob Jackson, the Imagineers' PR man, how such a thing could happen. He said someone had accidentally left a press kit somewhere where a *Sentinel* reporter had found it. How could that happen?

Well, it didn't. Years later, although no one ever confirmed the story, it became clear that *Sentinel* publisher Martin Anderson, who was also a prominent civic leader, had been informed of the project months ahead by Sun Bank president Billy Dial. Dial warned him that if the word got out ahead of time, the project would be impossible. I suppose that kind of thing could not happen on newspapers today, but if Anderson had not agreed, there would not be a Walt Disney World in the Orlando area today. By the time I heard the story, Anderson was dead so I never had a chance to ask him. My Disney friends who might have known ain't talking.

In return for Anderson's silence, Walt, I believe, had agreed that the *Sentinel* would get an exclusive on the first story. Thirty years later, *Sentinel* editors criticized Anderson's secrecy. He never told any of them and never admitted that he knew in advance.

I also think Anderson may not have been aware that Emily Bavar was going on the trip to Disneyland and may have been surprised by her first story. His weekend editors probably didn't even mention it before they ran it as "just another rumor."

I have another suspicion that after the story, Anderson talked to Disney people and got their permission to run the later story. By then the company had completed purchasing most of the critical parcels in the twenty-eight thousand acres they acquired originally through a series of dummy companies. They paid about $5.5 million for the twenty-eight thousand acres. Much of it, however, was unusable swampland, which is preserved today as an environmentally protected part of the property. Soon, adjacent parcels sold for hundreds of thousands of dollars but would not have been worth a swamp buggy had it not been for Disney's massive investment.

Emily Bavar became a hero because of her nose for news. An annual award for journalistic excellence on the *Sentinel* staff was named for her. Anderson sold his paper to the Chicago Tribune Company two years later. Many years afterwards there was a movement among the new editors of the paper to change the name of the Bavar award "since the paper should have had the story all along."

❦

Walt had been offered land in the New York Meadowlands World's Fair site, in North Carolina, near West Palm Beach and elsewhere. The others were too frigid to permit year round operation of things like the *Jungle Cruise*, Walt thought, and land in South Florida was far too expensive. A concept for an indoor Disney park in St. Louis, Missouri was dropped when surrounding landowners tried to exploit it mercilessly.

One Orlando area real estate land company had assembled about twenty thousand acres, which were offered to the unknown buyer. Jack Sayers, the head of corporate alliances and member of the Disneyland Operating Committee, told me how Walt had flown over the site in the company plane, looked down on that little sand island in the middle of Bay Lake and said, "That's going to be Tom Sawyer Island. Let's buy it."

When he told Roy he wanted to buy twenty thousand acres, the older brother said, "What in the hell are we going to do with twenty thousand acres?"

Walt's answer ended the argument.

"Wouldn't you like to have twenty thousand acres around Disneyland right now?"

He wanted enough land to avoid the problems of visual intrusion that he had battled in Anaheim for years. Developers wanted to build high-rise office buildings and hotels that would have been seen from inside the park. Can you imagine looking at pristine forests along the Rivers of America and seeing a big old glass-sided modern monster in the background?

Disneyland finally won the argument when the Anaheim City Council voted appropriate height restrictions. Walt also hated the fact that Disney got screen credit when some of the small motels up and down Harbor Boulevard started flirting with sleaze. Walt also disliked the ugly forest of neon signs that grew up all around the park.

In recent years, with construction of Disney's California Adventure next door to the original park and with cooperation of the city government and surrounding Anaheim property owners, overhead power lines were removed, standardized signage was required and the boulevards around the park were beautified. Walt would have been pleased.

With construction of Walt Disney World still five years away, I continued working at Disneyland following the Walt Disney World announcement. As I had during the first years, I continued working closely with Disneyland's Head Photographer Charlie Nichols, trying to get new angles for pictures that would best convey the feeling of people having fun in the park. Charlie was an old International News Service photog so he knew good news pictures. He had one idea. I had a different one. Usually we would compromise and wind up with a better picture than either one of us visualized in the beginning.

It was always a struggle, after eight or ten years, to come up with new angles on the Castle, for instance.

Invariably, visiting photographers on assignment to shoot the parks would arrive saying, "Now I don't want pictures of the Castle. It's just too much of a cliché, and it's been used everywhere."

So they would shoot for two days and would just be going up Main Street for the last time when they would decide to shoot one shot, just for the hell of it. And of course, that was frequently the one that got used.

When I first began working at Disneyland, a side benefit was being able to use my own children as volunteer models for "people having fun" publicity shots. Daughter Janet was six years old at the time. Son Scott was just past four. They were thrilled to have Daddy go to work at their favorite place in the world, although Scott was a little disappointed when he learned I wouldn't be wearing a white suit and selling ice cream on Main Street.

But he proudly pointed out to visiting relatives that my office was in City Hall, right next to "the potty." My favorite picture of them is sitting with a group of other youngsters surrounding Walt Disney during a "story-telling" session in front of Sleeping Beauty Castle. The photo was taken during the filming of a TV commercial for the *Wonderful World of Color.*

Other pictures we used included the kids riding *Dumbo* or *Flying Saucers* or Janet dressed to match her idol walking hand in hand with Alice in Wonderland in front of Sleeping Beauty Castle. Both were beautiful blondes.

Many of the Disney adventures presented a real challenge when it came to getting good stock photographs because they were inside. They were lighted for dramatic effect by Disney Imagineers to be seen, not photographed, and viewed from only certain angles as the guest would see them. I spent weeks with Charlie photographing *Pirates of the Caribbean*. Each of the many scenes was a lighting nightmare. Of course, we tried our best to get guest faces into the shot while showing what they were seeing as they rode along in flat-bottomed boats. That's pretty tough without mirrors.

Helping Charlie photograph *Pirates* was my first introduction to Ub Iwerks, down from the studio to arrange lighting for a TV special on the *Pirates*.

It was a year before I discovered Ub was more than a nice old guy who moved lights around. He was a true Disney legend. Iwerks was an inventive genius who gave Walt his first job drawing "Ladies Remove Your Hats" lantern slides for movie theaters in Kansas City. He was also the one who followed Walt to California to do animation on little things like *Steamboat Willie*. Walt would sketch a few characters to give the idea, but Ub was the one who did the animation.

Ub was a partner in Disney Brothers studio early on but later left because, he said, the pressure of big business was just "too much." And there were creative differences with Walt that he didn't mention. He returned to the company in 1940 to help develop new equipment and optical techniques used in many films, but he wanted no titles and no executive responsibilities. He just wanted to tinker around and help invent things. I understood Iwerks was instrumental in applying Xerox transfers of animators' pencil drawings to the cels instead of having them traced by ink and paint artists. It saved a bundle.

Soon after Walt's death we had lunch with Ub at WED Enterprises where he was helping develop new attractions for the future Walt Disney World. The lunch with Ub came during a training program called OD (Organizational Development), started in 1966 to prepare many of us for management roles when we would be moved to Florida. We had lunch with other key Disney people from animation, Imagineering, music, legal, maintenance, records and merchandising — all aspects of the company.

The "curriculum" included meetings and dinners with top management directors Card Walker and Donn Tatum. Our seminar group asked such impertinent questions as "Which of you will succeed President Roy O. Disney when he decides to retire?" (Both, at different times, became president and chairman of the company after Roy's death.) We had sessions with presidents of other major corporations like Bank of America. We were also scheduled to have lunch with Roy, but it was cancelled at the last minute.

The most fascinating of all the OD sessions was that luncheon at WED Enterprises, later Walt Disney Imagineering, with Ub Iwerks when he told about the night they first combined sound with cartoon animation.

The year was 1928, soon after Warner Brothers released *The Jazz Singer*, the first talking picture. It revolutionized movies, but when Walt first suggested using it for animated movies, many said it would not have the same impact with "cartoons."

As he related the story, Ub had just finished animating ninety seconds of *Steamboat Willie* starring Mickey and Minnie Mouse. It was actually Walt's third attempt at developing a "short" subject with Mickey as the star to replace the successful *Oswald the Lucky Rabbit*. Distributors had claimed all rights to *Oswald* and hired away many of the Disney animators. The first Mickey films were silent. Walt was unable to find a buyer.

The work had to be done in complete secrecy, so the new work was shifted to a makeshift workshop in Walt's garage. Walt's wife,

Lilly, and Roy's sister-in-law, Hazel Sewell, did the ink and paint-ing work transferring drawings to celluloid.

After everyone had left the Disney Brothers Studios for the day, Ub, Roy and his wife plus Walt and Lilly came in to try out the first ninety seconds of *Steamboat Willie*. With them were two assistants, Johnny Cannon and office boy Wilfred Jackson. They hung a sheet in the middle of the office and projected on that.

Roy ran the projector inside a glass-enclosed cubicle to reduce noise interference while Ub, Walt and Wilfred stood at a micro-phone behind the bed sheet. The challenge was to match voices and music with the film. Ub played a washboard and slide whistle. Can-non furnished sound effects. Jackson, the only musician in the crowd, played "Turkey in the Straw" on his harmonica. Walt pro-vided brief dialogue in his Mickey Mouse voice. It looked like the voice was coming from Mickey and the sound from instruments on the film.

They ran the brief piece of film time after time, getting more excited with each showing until well after midnight. At least that's how I remember Ub's story.

One other memorable part of OD sticks in my mind. We were re-quired to don the costume of a Disney character and parade down Main Street. I chose Pluto and was having a ball prancing along us-ing my big paws to shake hands with kids until we got down toward the end of Main Street. I suddenly discovered that playing character roles required more than just lively acting ability. It required a lot of breath. After all that prancing I was totally out of it. I had to stag-ger to a backstage gate and get "off stage" before I disgraced the character.

I was perhaps the oldest of the group going through OD, but that didn't prevent the others from kidding me for running out of wind. I was usually pretty windy.

Chapter 9

$\mathcal{I}$t was an unremarkable day in early December in 1966, nearly four years after my first day on the job. Christmas decorations were already up on Main Street, which always looked like a page out of Dickens' *Christmas Carol* at that time of year. Admiral Fowler called Eddie Meck and me to his office to break the news.

We had no warning that Walt was ill. A few weeks earlier, Walt had presided at an Imagineering press conference showing off plans for the forthcoming *Haunted Mansion*. He didn't look well, but said he was just getting over the flu. We learned later Walt had gone in to the hospital across the street from the Studio for a neck pain — an old polo injury, he thought — when the cancer was discovered. It was never revealed publicly even years after his death. Only four or five family members were told of the seriousness of the illness.

Walt wanted no big funeral like those of Marilyn Monroe and Clark Gable that shortly before had turned into media circuses. While the press and the world were waiting for word of a funeral, Walt was already buried in a private plot at Forest Lawn, causing a lot of stupid speculation about cryogenic freezing that continued for years.

On that suddenly-bleak December morning, at about ten o'clock, Joe Fowler said simply Walt had died and "the family has asked that no news photographers and TV cameras be allowed to come into the park."

The day was to go on as if nothing had happened. No announcements were made. No flags were lowered to half-staff except at the usual retreat ceremony at the end of the day when a brief acknowledgement of the death was made, mostly to a few cast members who had gathered. It was just outside my office door.

As Walt said in the opening dedication, this was a happy place, *"a source of joy and inspiration to the world."* He would not have wanted to have guests enjoying their day saddened by his death. Fortunately, attendance was light that day as was usual in early December.

Years later we were criticized for not lowering flags to half-staff in periods of national mourning. Somehow I felt if we hadn't done it for Walt, we shouldn't need to do it for anyone.

So we were not to allow reporters into the park to seek comments from guests about the death, not to allow camera crews inside the park. Something of a challenge for a young publicist! It was my task to go to the front gate all day and tell newspeople like veteran CBS correspondent Terry Drinkwater they were not welcome, at least not with a camera. That was tough to do in a public place even in those days. It would be a lot harder today.

I apologized. As an ex-reporter I understood his frustration, but I told Terry and others that until my orders were changed, they would have to restrict themselves to a quick look around. No cameras, no interviews.

Not surprisingly, they were persistent and many stayed around until late in the day when we were given permission to allow a limited amount of filming and interviews as guests were leaving. Most guests were not aware, although cast members certainly had learned through the grapevine within minutes of Walt's leaving.

For days, around the world, editorials, cartoons and newscasts assessed the great loss the world had suffered. Perhaps it should have been completely devastating for us Disneylanders, but it wasn't. Somehow Walt's inspiration was still with us. We felt we must go on as before because Walt would have wanted it that way. The park never closed, never became a sad place for guests.

One photographer, who worked for United Press International, saw an advance alert on the wire that day and promptly called his broker to sell his Disney stock. Like many others, he thought with Walt gone the company would go down hill fast. As a matter of fact, the stock went up immediately, as Wall Street figured the company's library of animated films would be sold at a big profit.

Perhaps the most amazing thing about Walt Disney is the fact that his influence and inspiration have lasted more than forty years past his death, pushing his company's growth beyond what even he might have imagined. I know of no other man whose personality has continued to inspire so many for so many years. As he said, "Disneyland will continue to grow as long as there is imagination left in the world."

Walt had many good friends among the press in Los Angeles, especially movie columnists like Hedda Hopper and Bob Thomas, the Hollywood correspondent for Associated Press. Bob later authored the official biography of Walt Disney, the only one of many that I thought accurately described the Walt Disney I knew. When we talk about Walt, both Bob and I get a little misty-eyed.

Others, like Richard Schickel, movie critic for *Time*, tried to get permission from the Disney family to write a biography and, when turned down, quickly went away and tried to find and interview all the people who had had a falling out with Walt. Schickel's book and others, I thought, were not only unfair but inaccurate, by lots.

The other half of the Disney brothers' team, Roy O. Disney, had been prepared to retire before Walt's death but stepped into the breach, promising to stay until Walt Disney World was up and running.

I first met Roy in April 1969 when hundreds of travel writers and newsmen were invited to see for the first time what we planned to build in Phase I of the Florida Project — a Magic Kingdom park, five hotels and two golf courses. Construction was already underway. It was my first time in Florida.

᭙

Several marketing, guest relations and publicity cast members like me had been loaned to the Florida Project for the press introduction. I flew in the company plane to Chicago and Cleveland to pick up some of our special press guests and bring them to Orlando. We set up tents at the Ramada Inn in Ocoee, west of Orlando, to display scale models of the project. Roy and Donn Tatum held a press conference in a nearby theater to show movies Walt had made before his death outlining the huge undertaking.

We took the press out to the site to see a big hole in the ground, which would be the Seven Seas Lagoon. More than seven million cubic yards had been dug from what had been a swampy area, hauled with giant earthloaders and stacked up where the Magic Kingdom would be built on the north shore of the man-made lagoon. It stayed in place for more than a year so it could compress into a solid building site before the excavation of tunnel and basement areas began.

By the time of the press showing, a wide trench had been dug down the middle of the earth-fill where tunnels called "utilidors" would provide underground access throughout the park. Through the utilidors, merchandise and food were delivered. Cast members were costumed and made their way through the tunnels before coming up in their themed work places. The tunnel system included dressing rooms, a cast cafeteria, maintenance facilities and a computer room from which all of the Audio-Animatronics shows were controlled.

Only a week before the 1969 press conference, I had been taken on my first tour of the property, riding slowly in a jeep over dirt trails for what seemed like a hundred miles. I kept saying, "When are we going to see the construction site?"

Bay Lake still had water in it, although it was later drained, scraped clean and refilled. While it was empty, white sand was hauled in to create beautiful beaches which served a double purpose — as a recreation area and to separate the lake from the swamp on the east side which had been the source of the lake's dark brown color. After refilling, it was a beautiful blue lake.

Seven Seas Lagoon was just a dry man-made lake bed at the time of the press event. When it was dug, three raised areas were left to become islands. During its two years as a dry hole, the islands sunk about six feet, so dirt was added. But when it was refilled, they raised back up again like floating islands.

Admiral Joe Fowler was thrilled during the digging of the lagoon when a fresh-water spring was discovered on the west side, thrilled until he learned that when it was refilled the spring would act like a drain in a bathtub. It had to be plugged up with concrete.

By the time of the press gathering, engineers had completed a forty-five-mile system of water control channels with automatic locks at regular intervals to maintain environmentally appropriate water levels throughout the property. I thought that meant draining the land to make way for the parks and resorts. Not so, I discovered. The locks were regulated to retain water during wet periods and allow the land to dry out during the dry season of the year, replicating Mother Nature.

When local residents found that Disney planned to operate the park, even at night, on land surrounded by pine forests and mosquito-filled swamps, they predicted it couldn't be done.

"The bugs will eat you alive the minute you turn on the lights," they said.

But acting through the Reedy Creek Improvement District (RCID), Disney found environmentally sound ways to control mosquitoes and other bugs and re-engineer large areas of the property to make way for hotels, parks and all the other things to come.

RCID was created by the Florida legislature as a taxing district to provide necessary utilities and services to this whole new kind of urban development. The district was supported entirely by taxes on the Disney property. RCID also developed utility lines, a central power station, environmental test facilities and a distribution station, a Fire Department, road system, a model building and safety code and all the other necessary infrastructure. Much of this was in place by the time the press came to look in 1969, although major shops for construction and maintenance were yet to be started.

Around the Seven Seas Lagoon for the press event large weather balloons were tethered to show the height and location of Cinderella Castle, the Contemporary and Polynesian hotels and other landmarks. It was hard even for us insiders to imagine what would be there two years later as we surveyed the site with the press standing on top of the berm that would carry railroad tracks around the Magic Kingdom.

By that time, antique steam engines had been purchased in Mexico and brought to Tampa for complete rebuilding, with Walt's old model-train helper Earl Vilmer in charge. He tore down each of the three forty-year-old engines and used them as molds and patterns to make all new parts.

Along with the rest of the Magic Kingdom, Admiral Fowler was personally overseeing the construction of two paddlewheel steamboats and fifteen fiberglass submarines in a Tampa yacht building yard. A dry dock was built in the North Service Area for continuing maintenance in years to come. Monorail beams were being poured in Seattle and Martin-Marietta's missile plant just up the road from the Disney property was assembling monorail trains in its large machine shops.

Landscape chief Bill Evans had been growing his eucalyptus, redwood and tropical jungle trees for a year in nurseries east of the park site. Other temporary warehouses and shops in the surrounding area were leased for building other components pending completion of Walt Disney World's own extensive woodworking, plastics, plumbing and electrical shops and warehouses.

All this was moving forward even as Roy O. Disney was outlining the details of the project's first phase at the 1969 press event in Orlando. When the event was concluded, all of the Californians gathered at a company cottage in the new Bay Hill Golf Course subdivision to celebrate.

Roy, looking like a godfather, was seated in a large wicker lawn chair in the backyard overlooking Lake Butler. The cast included several executives planning the new project and our corps of Disneyland tour guides, mostly very pretty young ladies in Scotch-plaid kilts and red vests, gathered around Roy. He was smiling with totally paternalistic pride.

I thought, "Right now, this is Walt Disney World. This is the new company. Soon there will be thousands more of us. But for now, we're it."

Three months later, I was back in Orlando with my wife and children. We flew down on Walt's plane, the one he bought for the World's Fair projects, to see if we wanted to make the move to Florida. I was offered the job as Publicity Manager, which meant my salary would jump from $175 to $200 a week. And a *manager* was pretty big stuff in those days when the only thing higher was a director. That's not true today.

Actually, since we didn't plan any advertising or promotion, publicity would carry the load of marketing the whole place and arranging press coverage for the grand opening. So it seemed an important job. (I was promoted to "Director of Publicity" following the opening of Epcot, eleven years later. By then, there were many who had been promoted to vice president positions, but I always wanted to stay in publicity and would have had to move to a broader role in marketing to move up another notch.)

That first time when we came to Orlando to look over the new job offer, we landed on a blazing hot July day. The humidity wasn't a bit over ninety-eight percent. We stayed in a company "cottage" at Bay Hill which was the plushest housing development around. It had a championship golf course later acquired by Arnold Palmer. That appealed.

We toured the town, investigated housing, talked with local folks about schools and managed to get over to Cape Kennedy for the moon shot. Gretta and the kids watched from nearby New Smyrna Beach. Our public relations guy, Sandy Quinn, was the first marketing person sent to Florida. (PR is different from publicity in

Disney-speak.) Sandy arranged for himself and me to sit at the press site at Cape Kennedy, directly in front of President and Mrs. Johnson, a big thrill. The roar was expected. The earthquake that came with the take-off was not.

The astronauts landed on the moon three days later, on my forty-sixth birthday. Now there's an omen!

Gretta and I decided a slower paced community would be good for the kids, who were ready to enter junior high school. But it meant selling the California house, moving, and figuring out a place for my eighty-year-old mother-in-law (she moved in with us.) Besides, I had loved California since I first saw it as a soldier in WWII.

But the prospects of this new job were just too good to pass up. The kids liked the lakes and water skiing.

I was hooked. I went back to Anaheim and moved my office into a backlot trailer with Bob Phelps, who headed costuming, and started writing stories about what the new resort would be. But I really never realized just what a mammoth project it would become.

By December, we had made another trip to Florida, bought a lot, picked a builder and put our California house up for sale. I was on my way to New York to make my first contacts with the big-time magazine and newspaper travel editors. On the way to the airport, Gretta and I decided to give up smoking, four packs a day for me with about half of them burning up beside the typewriter while I was writing, a crutch I guess.

I threw my cigarettes into a waste bin and flew all the way to the Big Apple, eight hours on a prop plane, gripping the arms of my seat and strangling for a cigarette. I never smoked even one again. I knew if I did I was lost.

In New York, I looked up my old friend Horace Sutton. I had gone with him and his family for a memorable tour of Disneyland years before. I took the kids on the *Matterhorn Bobsleds* ride when Horace and his wife were too chicken to try a "roller coaster." That started our family friendship. Horace was perhaps the best-known travel columnist in the country and was also the executive editor of Norman Cousin's *Saturday Review*. I talked to a score of other New York writers and editors in a week, including top editors like Caskie Stinnett at *Holiday*, Pat Carbine at *Look*, an old Missouri classmate John Mack Carter at *Good Housekeeping*, plus travel editors at *Mc-Call's*, *Redbook*, *Glamour*, the *Daily News* and others.

In Washington, I met new "friends," travel editors Maury Rosenberg at the *Post* and Chick Yarborough at the *Star* as well as several editors at *National Geographic* who had worked on the Walt Disney profile six years earlier. All were interested in finding out more about the new project.

Back in Anaheim, I sent out letters and made other contact trips, including a first visit to the Radio and Television News Directors Association convention in Detroit, which began a whole series of long-lasting friendships with TV journalists. I spent many hours at WED Enterprises watching them put together scale models and mock ups of adventures being prepared for Florida, including the hilarious *Country Bear Jamboree*. Marc Davis, once a top film animator at the studio, was in charge of designing the musical show. It was an instant hit after opening. Marc looked to me a lot like Big Al, the overweight star of the show. I loved watching him work. His was one show not already at Disneyland.

I hired an assistant, Duffy Myers, a former newspaper reporter, to stay in California and continue that work for another year while I moved on to set up shop in Florida.

In July of 1970, Gretta and I loaded up the Global Van, piled the family in one car and shipped the other, made a last chance swing through Grand Canyon and Jackson Hole and arrived just as our new house was being completed. We chose to move to Maitland, twenty-five miles away from my job, rather than settling in Bay Hill or nearby Windermere where many other Disney executives were building their homes. Very few services or schools existed in the Disney World end of the county. It seemed better for me to commute than for the rest of the family to suffer long rides to schools, grocery stores, doctors and libraries.

Before there was Walt Disney World there was a lot of emptiness, much of it uninhabitable swamp land. Once-brown Bay Lake was drained and refilled with clear water. The beautiful Seven Seas Lagoon encircled by monorail beams was created just to the west. While much of the tropical forest remains as it was then, four magnificent resort hotels and the Magic Kingdom now overlook the shores of the two lakes. (Courtesy of the Orange County Regional History Center.)

Chapter 10

$\mathcal{B}$eginning well before my move to Florida, we began developing press releases and story ideas to arouse even more public interest in Walt Disney World.

Some of our first good feature stories came from Bill Evans, Walt's fabulous landscape man, who was the first Disney builder to move to Florida. Trees take time. Bill loved his trees. He was the kind of guy who would walk up and give a sapling a gentle hug as he lowered it into the ground. They seemed to grow better after that. He tested California redwoods, which didn't do too well, and a dozen varieties of eucalyptus, which did. He figured out how to install gas-fired blowers to keep tender tropical plants alive in the *Jungle Cruise* during the occasional Florida freezes.

I began touring the planning office and construction sites, looking for stories. By early 1970, on frequent cross-country visits, I was able to walk down Main Street. Basic buildings were in place, but their facades were missing. I talked to steel workers erecting beams for Cinderella Castle. They were amazed by all the shapes and sizes of steel they had to put in place.

"Damnedest thing I ever saw," said one.

The castle foundations ran down two floors and the steelmen were at the bottom having lunch when I arrived.

They were among the many rare artisans who made good story material. Bud Washo, head of the Disneyland Staff Shop, brought a handful of expert craftsmen from Disneyland to teach a hundred more plasterers how to turn fiberglass and concrete into "ancient stones" for the castle walls and archways or for jungle ruins or frontier forts. ("Staff" is an old movie studio term referring to plaster molds and carvings.) In the rural crossroads town of Dr. Phillips nearby, Bud set up shop in an old fertilizer storage shed where the first decorative components for the castle were shaped and molded.

Other pieces of the project were being fabricated all over the world, including monorail beams in Seattle. The beams had to be shipped across the country, but were too long for a single rail car. Two cars were used for each beam, anchored only at each end for when the train went around curves. They were hauled from a railhead in Orlando on trucks with detached trailers, sort of like a hook and ladder fire truck.

Fortunately for us, many good construction workers had just finished building the Vehicle Assembly Building and other NASA structures at Cape Canaveral and were available. One of them would crawl out onto the steel arms forming the limbs of the *Swiss Family Treehouse* and place each leaf-covered branch in the proper hole. They called him "the squirrel." While he adjusted, art directors below would tell him which way to turn each of the five hundred thousand leaves. That, too, made a good feature story.

Early on, we sent photographer Bill Spidle from Disneyland to create a photographic record of the thirty-month job. Workmen drained Bay Lake to remove waters turned brown by tannic acid from the surrounding cypress trees. It was refilled with well water to create a clear blue lake. Bill never forgot being stranded in a rowboat barely afloat in the only remaining pool at the center of the lake. The pool was full of rattlesnakes.

After months of pile-driving on the lake shores, the Contemporary Resort Hotel elevator shaft began to rise in a continuous concrete pour. I remember going to New York on a Friday, when the shaft was up about ten feet. I came back in a week. The tower was ten stories high and workmen were inserting stairs. I climbed those stairs too many times, but the view was worth it. Sometimes newsmen went with me. You could see Cape Canaveral fifty miles away.

The A-shaped Contemporary was built like a bridge by U.S. Steel Corporation, using I-beams to create a skeleton frame for pre-fabricated guest rooms arriving from the other side of the property. Rooms for both the Polynesian and Contemporary hotels were built in a factory created especially for the job, completely assembled with walls, floors, plumbing, air conditioning and sliding-glass doors in place, then trucked across the property at thirty miles an hour, lifted by crane and slid into place in the main tower building like drawers in a bureau. It was part of the EPCOT concept for innovative construction.

The process was an experiment that worked, but only when the rooms could be hauled on private roads. They were too wide to travel on public highways on a regular basis so hoped-for applications elsewhere never happened. At the Polynesian Village Hotel and in the three-story wings of the Contemporary, the steel framed rooms were simply stacked on top of each other like big boxes with connecting hallways constructed on site. Workmen then connected wires and pipes to the main lines, added carpets and the hotels were ready. Even some furniture was in place.

Monorail trains ran through the fifth floor of the A-shaped tower building, riding on rectangular concrete beams overlooking the restaurants and shops on the fourth floor concourse. Hurricane-proof glass panels covered either end of the Grand Canyon atrium concourse. Six-inch-thick skylights dotted the ceiling. A magnificent mural by one of Walt's favorite artists, Mary Blair, was installed on the walls of the central elevator shafts, depicting Native American children at play. Passengers boarded the monorail trains inside the atrium and at three other stops along the mile-long track — at the main Transportation Center, alongside the Polynesian Village Hotel and at the Magic Kingdom.

It was amazing for me and for a limited number of press visitors to watch it grow so fast. We brought small press groups to tour the site beginning in January 1970, a short time after opening a Pre-view Center on the eastern edge of the property. A million visitors, including newsmen from as far away as Norway, came to the center to see artists' concepts, motion pictures and scale models of what we were doing three miles away.

Until then, curious Floridians could only drive around the edges of the thirty thousand acres looking for ways to get in. The company lawyer, Phil Smith, with his wife and two children, moved into the only house on the site, leftover from cattle-raising days. He found himself on weekends standing guard at the gate near his house turning sightseers away.

General Joseph Potter, hired by Walt to supervise creation of the Reedy Creek Improvement District and its function of provid-ing roads, sewers and other utilities, set up his office in the Metcalf Building in downtown Orlando in 1969 along with the project's first public relations spokesman, Sandy Quinn.

General Potter, formerly Governor of the Panama Canal Zone, had been the second in command at the New York World's Fair. He also had a major role in overseeing Disney hotel construction. They had met while Walt was installing his four shows at the New York World's Fair.

By the time I moved to Florida in 1970, work had been com-pleted on forty-five miles of canals for water control, several roads were completed and other parts of the infrastructure were under-way. Work on the Magic Kingdom and the first two hotels was in full swing with construction workers crowding the site.

We continued bringing a very limited number of small groups of press from major cities throughout the East to build up aware-ness of the project.

I took one press group from Iowa through the site in the fall of 1970. It was a madhouse with half-built structures, dirt and mud everywhere and more than four thousand workers on site. One newsman was definitely *impressed* when a two-by-four blew off a pile of lumber and hit him on his hard hat. I knew then why we always insisted on hard hats.

I thought I had done a good job of showing the group just what this would be like in October, 1971, but found out later on the way back on the company plane the group decided unanimously that "There's no way they will finish next year." Other later groups came to the same conclusion. It was close.

There were plenty of humorous incidents during construction. Our Disney World motion picture cameraman, Al Aubiel, was documenting construction progress. He showed us the film of two carpenters moving a pile of lumber atop a large porch outside the Penny Arcade on Main Street. They carried it one piece at a time from one side to the other; then turned around and carried each piece back to the original spot.

Dave Langford, Orlando correspondent for United Press, who remained a friend for thirty years, wrote one of the funniest news stories during the frantic construction days at Walt Disney World. Dave's story gave a real insight into the character of Orange County as it was about to change into one of the nation's best-known metropolitan areas, mostly because of Disney.

The story was all about Johnny's Corner, where State Road 535 turned west. It was a dilapidated bar catering to hunters and fishermen going up what had been a little traveled road into woodlands and lakes. He stocked live bait and shotgun shells. There were pickled eggs and pigs feet, plus thick workmen's socks on the bar.

Now, however, Johnny's was the first place where five thousand workmen leaving the Disney construction site each day could get a bottle of beer. It was a bonanza. But the sudden prosperity was more than "Johnny" could stand.

Until now, ten cases of beer were plenty to supply Johnny's usual trade. Now, the beer received each Monday ran out by the end of the day. But Johnny really thought handling ten cases of beer was just about all the work he wanted to do in a week. Thirsty workmen complained but could do nothing but gripe and drive on for another ten miles.

Within months, Johnny sold out. The new owners set up saw horse tables in the front yard, stacked beer cases to the ceiling and made enough money in the next year to retire for life. They still kept pickled eggs on the bar until the property was sold to become a great big red and white Texaco gas station.

Almost all of the construction workers were men. Although a few women wearing orange vests started directing traffic on site, women in the construction trades were a rarity then.

We had a rule that women could come on the site during construction hours only if they wore slacks — no skirts — and solid shoes. Workmen could ignore even very pretty women in town, but let one in a skirt come into the construction site — shaboom!

Shortly before the October opening of Walt Disney World, we decided to risk a photographic fashion shoot, a layout on kids' clothes for *Parents Magazine*. It was one of several early nation-wide publicity opportunities. It had to be shot in July to be ready for the October issue. The pictures had to look like the park was finished, even though landscaping and parts of buildings were very much unfinished. So we shot in colorful little corners of the Magic Kingdom or close to finished portions, usually photographed after the end of construction each day.

Finally, to get more favorable lighting conditions, we were given permission to do a final set-up in Town Square around eight in the morning. Except for paving and landscaping, construction was mostly done in that area. I left an assistant to stay with the group. Later when more workmen arrived, the kids were still posing. Construction workers didn't pay much attention until a statuesque blond fashion coordinator finished dressing the kid models and suddenly appeared in Town Square wearing very short, very pink hot pants, which were very fashionable that year.

I got a frantic call from Joe Fowler.

"Get those people out of there. They've shut down the job!"

I raced out to correct our oversight. Work had come to a standstill. It didn't take a whole lot to distract workers as each day got hotter. The word had spread, bringing many from a block away.

Earlier that year, in January, we brought a group of press from Mexico City to Town Square to see the Resort taking shape. We set up lunch for them on the upper level platform of the Main Street Railroad Station during the workmen's lunch breaks. It was the first time we had ever tried to use a site in the park. We were handing out box lunches when Roy O. Disney decided to join us, a special treat for me. The Mexican editors talked about very little else for the rest of the trip.

My favorite picture of Roy is one I set up with him and Mickey Mouse on opening day, sitting cross-legged on a bench in front of City Hall. Twenty-five years later I posed his son, Roy E. Disney, in a similar crossed-legged position for our park anniversary publicity.

Perhaps the best pre-opening publicity opportunity came when *Look* decided to do a multi-page picture story. It had to be shot at least six weeks before publication. Although it was a month or so after the *Parents* shoot, the resort was still crowded with cranes, scaffolding and skip-loaders.

Focusing on limited portions, the *Look* crew managed to get finished-looking shots of Cinderella Castle and City Hall, masking out the un-landscaped grounds in front of them. We posed pretty girls at play on the beach across from the Contemporary Hotel while construction cranes dominated the skyline. The photographer hid them by placing his camera strategically behind a pair of palm trees.

His cover photo was a tight shot of Mickey Mouse with early-test fireworks bursting in a dark sky behind the famous Disney icon.

Two days after the soft opening weekend, we gathered more than half of the five thousand cast members at daybreak in front of Cinderella Castle for a *Life* photographer. All the Disney characters and the Magic Kingdom's colorful marching band posed in the front row, providing a colorful and spectacular mob-scene photograph. That one made *Life's* cover ten days before the October 25 Grand Opening.

Ten years later, we gathered twice as many, ten thousand cast members, filling all of Main Street for a similar *Life* spectacle shot. I stood beside the photographer on a high-lift with a bullhorn directing hand-waving cheers for the camera. Except for a few recognizable people and characters in the foreground, the picture was a great sea of faces. Few of the thousands on hand would be able to pick out their faces in the crowd. Again, the picture had to be shot in early morning to avoid interfering with park operations despite less than ideal daylight at that hour. We repeated those mob scene photos in several variations on later anniversaries.

Although builders had the Disneyland format to draw on, construction in Florida was very different. Mildew ate holes in walls in plasterboard and insulation in buildings along Main Street before air conditioning could be installed. Structures were designed to withstand 250-mile-an-hour winds, far stronger than even the most powerful hurricanes. Canopies and cooling fans to shield many outdoor waiting areas were even more necessary than in California, partly because of the more unpredictable weather.

Some techniques developed in California worked equally well in Florida. Walt had a habit of tabbing one individual for a particular job even if it was outside his normal duties and perhaps clearly outside of his expertise. He called it "naming the sheriff." The idea was adopted in Florida.

For example, shortly before the opening of Disney World, workers were ready to pour concrete for red-colored sidewalks on Main Street. No red coloring powder. It was delayed on Boston docks. The "sheriff's" job went to Marketing Director Jack Lindquist, later president of Disneyland. It was a Friday. "It must be here by Monday morning."

No problem. Jack flew to Boston, chartered a plane, supervised loading of the coloring powder despite having to get it done on the weekend and flew back with it. I'm not sure if he had to hold it in his lap. The concrete was poured on time.

Dick Nunis, then chairman of the Park Operating Committee, had the biggest sheriff's job of all, riding herd on fifty contracting firms and five thousand workmen. Neglecting his role as head of park operations, Dick took over for the final six months to make sure that construction got done on time. He was the guy out there with an S.O.B. painted on his hard hat, ordering, begging and pushing every crew in the place.

Nunis held meetings of his Park Operating Committee each weekday morning to review critical problems for that day. As the construction deadline neared, the meetings got to be earlier and earlier. Finally the call was for six o'clock.

When the chairman walked into the meeting room, he discovered committee members wearing pajamas and brandishing toothbrushes. He got the message. Subsequent meetings did not start until seven.

Construction crews also started early to beat the heat of the Florida summer, at least for part of each day. By August, however, they were working around the clock, three shifts and overtime. Come Labor Day, less than a month out from opening, union leaders told Dick, "Our guys have to have a break. We have to take the weekend off."

Reluctantly, Nunis agreed, deciding to use the time to test and run those attractions that could be operated. More importantly, he invited construction workers to come with their families to try out and enjoy the attractions. They all came.

Fathers proudly pointed to their individual accomplishments. When Junior turned to Father and said "Dad, you got to hurry up and finish this for me," well, you could see the workers swell with pride.

On Tuesday, the pace of construction doubled. Work went on with gusto and was finished enough to open as scheduled on October 1. Yes, there was no paint on basement walls. Offices over Main Street stores had bare bulbs on wires hanging from the ceilings and metal studs where walls would be, but the attractions were ready to go, except for a few in Tomorrowland.

The Polynesian Village Hotel was ready for guests October 1, although there was no hot water for Governor Askew's Friday morning shave. But the turnstiles were ready to turn for the first paid guests.

On Thursday, giant cranes still rose high beside the Contemporary Hotel, which would have spoiled the appearance for the first visitors. The offending cranes were taken down for the inaugural weekend. Where they had rested was covered, as if by magic, with bright green grass.

When the regular landscapers were too worn out to work through the night, Nunis himself hired a bunch of students from Rollins College to lay six acres of sod at the hotel. All night he walked around the site shouting, "Green side up!"

Those offending cranes went back up on Monday so workmen could get as much work done as possible before celebrity guests arrived. They stayed until the day before the Grand Opening in late October when the cranes came down for good. Actually, the hotel was not completely finished until the New Year, but enough rooms were done to accommodate Grand Opening guests and ceremonies in the Grand Canyon concourse on October 25.

For more than a month prior to October 1, we had declared a "press blackout," needing to avoid photography and press visits that could interfere with construction and wanting to build anticipation for the opening. During the same period, at the end of each work day, we brought in groups of community leaders, civic clubs and cast member families to give our new employees needed practice in operating the Magic Kingdom and its many attractions.

That's a neat trick — keeping the media out while one hundred thousand other people are passing through. We made it with only one or two journalists sneaking with other guests. Very little was written about what they saw.

Dick Nunis, who was Director of Operations at the time, got all excited one day during the blackout when he saw a car with large WDBO radio station call letters on the side heading up the entrance road. He stopped the driver, a local news director and a good friend of mine. Newsman Bob Martin explained his daughter had been invited to bring her family, including Bob. He promised to keep mum. Dick apologized and later became good friends with the newsman.

Meanwhile, on the eve of the first opening day, I conducted the weirdest press conference I ever held, "entertaining" a room full of eager but disgruntled, sometimes belligerent, reporters at the Hilton Inn South, ten miles from the site. We had to prepare them for the next morning, giving rules and advice for covering the event.

I had visited the press room we were building in the Polynesian a few minutes before heading out for the press briefing at the Hilton. It still had no wallpaper, no carpet, only bare bulbs hanging for lights, no phones, no desks. Frankly, it was a mess. I was told not to worry, everything would be fine.

We had not invited any press for that opening day, planning to bring in travel writers and TV crews from around the nation during the next three weeks, before the Grand Opening.

But major publications didn't wait for an invitation. Present at that raucous September 30 press conference in the Hilton Inn South as I attempted to answer a thousand questions were *Time, Newsweek,* the *New York Times, Washington Post, Miami Herald, Cocoa Today, Orlando Sentinel,* all three local TV news stations, plus crews from Tampa, Miami and Jacksonville and too many more to recall.

Needless to say they were eager and a little angry because we had kept them away from the site for the past six weeks. They actually begged for an early morning pre-opening tour to see final preparations.

"Okay," I conceded, "I'll meet you at six a.m. at the Polynesian Village Hotel Pressroom."

One of my first hires at Walt Disney World was definitely one of the best. Louise Gerow began as a clerk typist, became my secretary a few years later, and left to take charge of the Walt Disney World Ambassador program. We still worked together on many projects until she "retired" in 1993.

Chapter 11

$\mathcal{T}$he night before the big day, I went to bed at the Hilton Inn South, leaving a wake-up call for 4:30 a.m. in order to check out and be on time to meet the reporters at the Polynesian Village. Wouldn't you know? The desk clerk forgot to call. I woke up at 4:45 with a start, panicked, threw on my clothes, grabbed my suitcase, jerked open the door of the lobby, yelled, "You SOB, you forgot to wake me up!" and threw my key sixty feet to the other end of the lobby. I guess I was sort of put out.

I arrived at the Polynesian by 5:05 and walked into the pressroom. Wallpaper was on the wall, carpet was installed and chandeliers were hanging. Desks were in place with phones ringing. My staff was all there, signing in the first arriving reporter.

The press gathered before dawn. We crossed the Seven Seas Lagoon by ferryboat to reach the Magic Kingdom entrance, walked down Main Street to see cast members hosing down the pavement and erecting banners, toured the entire park and returned to the Ticket and Transportation Center in plenty of time to see the first guests lined up for the opening.

October 1 was memorable in many ways from a publicity standpoint. In the days preceding, central Florida newspapers got into some kind of unplanned contest to see who could predict the highest number of guests for the opening. The build-up of public interest had been enormous.

I used to say when I first arrived in Orlando there were two kinds of people. There were those who thought this was another of those Florida real estate scams and nothing at all was being built out there in the swamp. And there were others who kept asking why we hadn't opened months earlier. All of them were waiting for dollar bills to come raining down out of the sky.

One paper predicted twenty-five thousand people for opening day. We had figured about ten thousand, but were not making any predictions publicly. We had scheduled it in what is traditionally the lightest vacation month of the year, on a Friday, the lightest day of the week. But we were really only guessing.

Another paper said fifty thousand, another one hundred thousand. Finally, *Cocoa Today*, being used to estimating crowds for the launches at Cape Canaveral, predicted two hundred thousand people. To make it worse, a veteran Reuters correspondent at the Cape picked up the story and moved it on her wire. Somehow a zero got added in transmission and all over Europe they read we were expecting two million people for the opening.

The Florida Highway Patrol made elaborate plans to handle a massive traffic jam. There were hundreds of people staying overnight in nearby roadside rest areas so they could be first in line when we began admitting cars up the one and only entrance road in the early morning.

Our executives began to worry.

"Maybe we were wrong."

Disney's Executive Vice President, Card Walker, and Operations Director, Dick Nunis, went up in a helicopter at five o'clock in the morning and looked up toward Orlando. Coming south down Interstate 4 were headlights as far as they could see.

"Good Lord, it's started already!"

But wait a minute. Those headlights were headed north up State Road 535 toward the employee entrance. It was our five thousand cast members coming to work.

By eight, it was clear that the press predictions were way off. There were several hundred cars in the parking lot and a thousand or so guests waiting at the front gate, but not a big mob.

At the gate, Marketing Director Jack Lindquist looked over the crowd waiting at the fourteen turnstiles and picked the one that would turn for the "First Visitor." His family would receive a guided tour, a night in the hotel and other favors, although that was not announced in advance. By "pure coincidence" Jack picked the one where a family of five handsome blond guests awaited, man, wife and three beautiful children.

So William Windsor, Jr. and his family were the ones mobbed by the cameramen as they came through the turnstiles for the official greeting and learned of their good fortune. The Windsors had slept in their car at the nearest roadside rest area to be among the first into the parking lot.

They were "overwhelmed" of course, but not enough to prevent William from coming to Lindquist later in the day to ask for coins to play the penny arcade.

After the ceremony, I returned to my crowded City Hall office to begin meeting other incoming press. A few minutes later, I was called to the Guest Relations desk out front to answer a phone. A woman's voice.

"Charlie," she said, "This is Helen. I'm ready to come to work."

"Pardon me, this is who?'

"Helen," she replied. "Remember, we rode down from Washington on the train last night — all night on the train — and you promised me a job in publicity."

"Not me," I said. "I haven't been out of Orlando in three months." I was too busy in that press conference at the Hilton Inn South.

"This is Charlie Ridgway?" Helen asked with a worried tone.

"Yes, but I certainly wasn't on a train yesterday."

"Oh, my God," were her last words as she hung up.

I hope she didn't pay too dearly for that job promise.

᳄

Publicity had been assigned offices upstairs in City Hall, as in Disneyland, convenient for news media. But it wasn't available for opening. Disney Imagineers still needed the office space to finish final construction of the park. So for two months after opening, our eight-person staff was relegated to a fifteen-by-fifteen-foot reception room on the ground floor, later used as a Guest Relations office. We moved from our trailer on the other side of the property the day before the opening.

We crowded eight desks into the room, so tight that to answer the phone on desks in the rear, you had to walk across the top of ones in front. Filing cabinets were in a hallway just outside. The crowding was eased slightly because for the first month part of our staff worked in the Polynesian Village pressroom and the rest were usually out in the park.

For October 1, local newspapers and TV stations had assigned every available reporter to cover each area of the resort. Tom Wilkenson from the *Orlando Sentinel* duly reported that Governor Askew had missed his shave because there was no hot water at the Polynesian.

Sports writer Jerry Green, then of *Cocoa Today*, was assigned to the Golf Resort, which had two unblemished eighteen-hole courses and a small club house. He arrived at dawn. A dozen eager attendants were waiting with tees and towels.

Came seven o'clock, there were no early golfers in sight. Of course, there was no way to reserve tee times in advance. Eight o'clock came, then nine o'clock, finally at ten the first player, all alone, arrived with golf clubs protruding from the front hatch of his beat up Volkswagen Beetle.

"Any chance of playing a round today?" he asked.

It must have been a lonely one.

At the close of the day, Jack Lindquist and Disney President Donn Tatum were on hand on the balcony at the Polynesian atrium for a press conference to sum up the opening. Attendance, they reported, was about ten thousand. (I think they counted a few of those cast members who were sailing around the lagoon in Sun Fish sailboats to make the place look alive.)

"That is what we expected," they said. But no one there believed them. The *New York Times* among others reported, "Disappointing opening."

Attendance continued to be relatively light except for the Grand Opening weekend, probably because we had invited half of Orlando to come out during those blackout preview days and people from far away waited for a holiday weekend.

Cocoa Today called me at home every night, usually after I went to bed, to get the attendance figures for the day. We soon decided to stop giving out attendance figures, but they kept trying. *Sentinel* reporters called too, but thank goodness it was usually during business hours.

We learned immediately after opening in Florida that afternoon rains were a way of life, very different from California where winter rains had a tendency to drizzle all day, sometimes resulting in early closing.

But in Florida the afternoon thunderstorms can end as quickly as they begin. And the minute they are over guests can't wait to ride. We learned to have a stack of very absorbent towels on hand to dry off the seats of hundreds of ride vehicles, trains and boats in a hurry.

We also learned that Florida's humidified heat requires a lot more air circulation, shade and inside, air-conditioned waiting areas. Many new ways were found to shelter guests from the sun. Later attractions were built with expanded cooled waiting areas.

Umbrellas and yellow plastic rain ponchos are big sellers during the summer. On suddenly cold days in winter we could barely put out enough sweat shirts. Folks just don't seem to expect weather to be other than ideal when they come to Disney parks.

❧

To avoid the disaster of Disneyland's Black Sunday, we had decided to have a series of press trips during the three weeks between opening day and Grand Opening. With just four publicists and four clerical cast members we had called hundreds of potential invitees, followed up with invitation letters, made airline and hotel reservations and all the rest of the arrangements needed.

The park established a separate office to handle arrangements for guests who were invited for the Grand Opening, but those preliminary press trips were all ours. There were about fifty journalists plus their wives in each group. Lodged at the Polynesian Village hotel, they included travel writers from newspapers and magazines plus television news reporters. Their itinerary included a day in the Magic Kingdom, a tour of the rest of the property, and time to enjoy sailboats and other recreation before what was supposed to be a gala evening luau complete with hula dancers on the Polynesian Village beach.

However, being October, it rained nearly every afternoon, which meant the set up for the luau was ruined — all six nights — as the beach was too wet for sitting. So every night we moved our luau inside to an upstairs balcony area overlooking the central atrium lobby. A little less glamorous, but dry.

Each night, Hawaiian dancers performed. Chefs paraded around the balcony carrying a large roasted pig with an apple in his mouth. Polynesian torch carriers led the parade. We never admitted the pig was really made of plastic, but my staff got pretty tired of seeing that same "pig" passing our tables night after night.

For the Grand Opening television special, a real pig was used at the luau and, for the first time in a week, there was no afternoon rain. It turned out to be a sparkling evening when the *Electrical Water Pageant* sailed across the Seven Seas Lagoon for the first time.

Another event on our Press Trip itinerary provided a moment of high humor for one of the groups. We took each group for a moonlight cocktail cruise on the elegant side-wheel steamboat that Admiral Fowler had supervised in construction. It created a glittering spectacle on the lake, with tiny white light bulbs around the rim of each deck.

This particular night, however, with the steamboat pilots still learning their way around Bay Lake, we ran aground on a sandbar called Treasure Island. At the time, it was completely deserted, although later it became Discovery Island bird sanctuary. A small sandy spit of land, it had only a few cypress trees and patches of undergrowth.

We came to a jarring stop. The pilot reversed engines and the paddlewheels churned. Nothing! He tried pushing back and forth. Still stuck in the sand! The Dixieland band on board began playing "When the Roll is Called Up Yonder" and other appropriate tunes.

"Everyone move to the back of the boat."

The paddles churned. The ship wouldn't budge.

"Everyone move to the front of the boat."

More churning!

"Women and children first," we yelled, reaching for another cocktail. Later our passengers accused us of planning the whole thing for dramatic effect.

A half-hour later, a pair of speedboats arrived to shuttle the group, six at a time, back to the Contemporary Hotel dock. I guess, without a load of passengers, the boat was able to back off the sandbar because it was gone the next day.

Press reaction to the opening events was generally very favorable although the negative comments about low attendance didn't help. Low attendance totals continued for six weeks. Disney Chairman Roy O. Disney, I heard through the grapevine, said if business didn't pick up by Thanksgiving, we were in trouble. Fortunately he lived to learn of giant crowds on Thanksgiving weekend. He had promised Walt on his deathbed he would not retire until he could get Walt Disney World up and running. He died unexpectedly of a heart attack a month after that Thanksgiving.

Thanksgiving became a traditionally heavy attendance time but nothing like that first one. Cars were backed up for miles. Every hotel room as far north as the Georgia border was filled. Roadside parks were full. The Disney parking lot had to be closed on Friday to prevent overcrowding in the park. It was the first holiday weekend when families could get away in large numbers. The boom was on!

Christmas week was even busier. Our fifteen hundred rooms in the Contemporary and Polynesian were booked up for a year. Before his death, Roy O. Disney had completed buying back the U.S. Steel interest in the hotels. It was his last gift to us. I can't imagine our execs having to run up to Pittsburgh every time they needed to repaint a room or adjust prices.

The five hotels on our property at Lake Buena Vista were nearly as full. For the next fifteen years, except during the 1973 gas crisis, guests had to call months ahead to get a reservation on property during busier times of the year.

We tried many new things during the first year or two after opening to make our guests' experience as smooth and trouble-free as possible. We even built a StolPort for short-take-off-and-landing planes to speed transfer from the airport to the hotels for those who would rather fly. Turned out it really didn't save much time because guests still had to transfer to a bus or van to go from the StolPort to their hotel. I flew it once in a strong wind and discovered I didn't like landing sidewise. When the airline that ran it went bankrupt for entirely unrelated reasons, the port was abandoned and never reopened. But the landing strip is still in use as a car park during major press events.

It wasn't until 1985, after Michael Eisner took over as Chairman and Chief Executive Officer, that we began catching up with demand with a massive construction effort that has brought the total inventory to more than thirty-four thousand hotel rooms, villas and campsites on property.

In the year following opening, when spring and summer vacation seasons were jam-packed and we frequently had to shut off the flow of private cars to curb overcrowding in the Magic Kingdom, finding a hotel room for visiting press — even important ones — was a tough task. That room shortage resulted in the only time I ever wrote a complaining letter to a major paper. An important writer from the *New York Times* called in the middle of 1972 seeking help in making a reservation at the Contemporary Hotel in August. After a week of arm twisting we arranged a reservation.

We warned writer Fred Ferretti that he would not be able to get into his room until after three in the afternoon because other guests were trying to cram in as much time in the Magic Kingdom as they could before checking out. Unlike most businessmen's hotels, we had almost no early check-outs.

Fred and family arrived at nine in the morning and demanded their room. The front desk called me. They did have a room but it could not be made up until much later. At my request, they let the reporter take his luggage to the room (instead of putting it in the lobby storage room) and suggested he visit the park until after three. He refused and instead sat fuming in his room until mid-afternoon waiting for someone to clean it. At least that is the way he wrote it in his story.

Six months later that story appeared, blasting Disney for its lousy hotel operations and also complaining that the castle was made of plastic, which it wasn't. The recorded bird songs and everything else was artificial, he reported. And besides, it was too hot and too crowded. No mention was made that the experience took place six months prior to the story's publication, during an opening period when we were struggling to improve operations, especially in the hotels. In the interim, we had made drastic changes in the hotel management. And by the time the story appeared things were operating much more efficiently.

Besides, Ferretti would never have been able to make a reservation at a Disney hotel that summer without the assistance of my office.

Another letter of complaint, not from me, went to a major paper when our London publicists wrote to the *London Times* editor, whom he knew, complaining about a story that spoke of Disney and his parks in rather insulting terms. He got a nice letter back. "Stuff it!"

Another problem for publicity, as with any office staff, is hiring the right people. I always tried to find people who had practical experience on newspapers, magazines, radio and TV stations rather than those from Public Relations agencies. Madison Avenue take note.

Before I retired, I was able to hire one of the nation's finest travel writers, Rick Sylvain, only because the *Detroit Free Press*, where he was Travel Editor, decided to have a nasty strike. Rick now runs the Walt Disney World print media relations department with the same kind of understanding of newspaper and magazine writers. Rod Madden, a former TV news director from Topeka, Kansas, who still handles the electronic media, gained his understanding of radio and TV people from the inside. Although things have become a bit corporate in recent years, I hope Rick and Rod will still have enough freedom to use their insider knowledge to carry on the Disney reputation with the media.

There were other travel writers, radio and TV news directors, magazine writers, freelance writers, TV reporters, sports writers and newspaper journalists on my staff. One had done TV network publicity, another public relations for the U.S. Air Force, but mostly they were news people. Most brought with them not only knowledge of the media from the inside, but personal contacts that were always helpful in building real friendships among newspeople.

They have a natural understanding of how reporters, editors and other newspeople think, what they want and how we can provide it for them. Some have gone on to higher jobs in the company. Some have left the company for better positions. But all of them made my job easy. Among them is a group who call themselves Charlie's Angels, the mostly young and attractive women I was lucky enough to hire. I make no apologies for that and certainly don't confess to being a dirty old man. Disney has always attracted young attractive people for its cast members because, let's face it, Disney is a great place to have fun, particularly for ambitious young people.

Like my own children, thousands of college students have helped pay for their education by working part time or seasonally at Disney resorts. The discipline required in terms of appearance and job performance is a never-forgotten lesson.

The training program developed by Walt and Van France in the early days turned into a vast human resources program called the Disney University. It develops textbooks, operating manuals, advanced training programs and the unique orientation for new cast members. In recent years, it has made a big business of holding training seminars for businesses from all over the world who want to know more about "the Disney Way."

At a time when many corporations were cutting back on their press contact people and relying more and more on agencies, we kept increasing our internal publicity staff to cope with the growing size and complexity of the Walt Disney World Resort. It seems hard for outsiders to understand the Disney Way, at least in the news media area.

In one notable test, we hired a big time New York PR agency to help when we were preparing to send several of our chefs for TV appearances in cities around the country to promote the many fine new restaurants that represented a major change in our food services initiated by Michael Eisner. We asked the agency to write promotional material for the chefs to take with them to attract TV and radio interviews and so that interviewers would have a better idea what to ask. We were too busy with a lot of other things to handle it, we thought, so it was a good time to test our do-it-yourself policies.

The agency's top dogs were very knowledgeable. But the sweet young ladies they sent to do the interviews and write the copy wouldn't know a feature story if they saw it running down the street, stark raving naked. Using their best Smith College English they wrote a biography of each chef. Only thing was, they forgot to include the fact that the chefs cooked at Walt Disney World, or anything about the restaurants where they worked. Close the oven and turn on the gas. We had to redo all the material.

The first tip I received from my veteran travel writer friends in 1963 came out of many boring press trips.

"When hosting a group of newspeople," they said, "don't treat them like travel agents. Above all, *don't sit them down for a sales pitch showing slides of all the things you are about to take them to see.* That's a death sentence. In fact, don't make sales pitches." I have used that advice ever since.

I always felt Walt Disney World, even more than Disneyland, was so different and complex it could not be adequately represented by someone who was not thoroughly familiar with the resort on a daily basis and loved it. We were inspired by our daily experiences in all parts of the resort, things like rubbing shoulders with guests and watching Disney characters enchant the crowds.

The publicity staff frequently included up to twelve staff members (publicists) plus an equal number of clerical people to maintain our mailing lists, handle phones and correspondence, sort and store clippings and broadcast reports and do a myriad of other jobs. That's a large number by today's standards, but it took all of them to keep up with the variety of publicity needs and opportunities. Today's media relations staff is even busier as the resort keeps growing.

New technologies like computers, cell phones, pagers, fax machines and finally the Internet made our jobs easier, and more complex at the same time. It took more technical know-how. But it still took the right people to make it all work. And they really had to love the place.

At Walt Disney World's opening, the publicist and clerical group was just eight people, but as we added more attractions, more parks and broader publicity efforts on a world-wide basis, the added help was needed. I frequently jumped in myself to assemble press kits and do other necessary grungy chores, always feeling I would never ask a secretary or staffer to do anything I was not willing to do myself, particularly under pressing deadlines. I'm not sure that is considered very managerial these days, but it worked for me.

Louise Gerow, the second clerical helper I hired and later my secretary before she went on to take charge of our Walt Disney World Ambassador program, reminded me of one night during construction when we put together the press kits for the first of many incoming press groups. Our trailer, parked in the middle of a sandy field, barely had enough desks to go around and no other furniture. Without tables, we sat on the floor in an empty room and assembled the kits. There were four of us who made up the staff at the time plus Louise's three teenage children who volunteered to help well into the night.

The resort also had its own photographers. Until they became more concentrated on advertising and brochure photography, our staff of seven or eight photographers spent most of their time on publicity pictures. We had a complete photo lab and technicians to develop our own prints and slides. Their lab was in the "basement" under Main Street, U.S.A. The sound of horse-drawn streetcars rolling overhead reverberated among the enlarging machines and developing tanks.

Until the late 1980s, publicity was still the principle marketing arm for the resort, although word-of-mouth and television programs such as the Christmas and Easter parades were probably far more important than anything we did in the Publicity Department in building Walt Disney World's world-wide reputation.

Along with cast members from other offices, our staff was called on to take part in "Cross-Utilization" during busy Christmas or Easter vacation times. Because part-time cast members often came from local schools with different vacation breaks than those in other parts of the country, Disney World couldn't get enough added help at critical times.

Cross-U helped us maintain services. Staff members, managers and clerical people from backstage areas were trained to stuff hamburgers, inspect restrooms and bus tables. That was my favorite. It gave me a chance to meet and talk with scores of families from around the world, ask them where they lived, and listen to their tales of travel, mainly at the park.

The resort also recruits college students in many parts of the country to work during Easter, Christmas and summer vacations.

I've tried to count the number of grand openings, attraction openings, birthdays, parades, major announcements of upcoming projects and other major press events in which I had a hand. The nearest I can come is more than 110 different ceremonial and press events in California, Florida and France, and I'm sure I missed counting several.

One of the more memorable openings came in 1975 when we began a year-long America on Parade for the nation's Bicentennial. Mickey, Goofy and Donald led the way, costumed as Minutemen, complete with bandaged heads, playing the fife and drums.

Among the invitees were Brady Black and his wife. Brady, then editor of the *Cincinnati Enquirer*, had been interested in Disney parks for a long time. They brought their draft-age son along. I knew they had been worried about the young man as had many of my friends with their sons. He had been against the war and even threatened to burn his draft card.

The four of us watched the whole parade. I wasn't close enough to hear, but I saw her son lean over and speak into his mother's ear. A few minutes later she told me, with tears in her eyes, what he had said.

"Mom, this country isn't so bad after all."

"I never thought he would say anything like that," Mrs. Black said.

I've often thought about the part that wars played in Walt's life and his work in movies and outdoor entertainment. His first drawings as an almost adult were when, as a sixteen-year-old ambulance driver, he went to France in World War I and started drawing cartoons for the amusement of wounded soldiers and his comrades.

During World War II, Walt and Roy lost most of their studio's money making training films, insignias and morale boosting pictures for the armed forces. As far as I can remember, Disney really never made any war pictures, with the exception of some Revolutionary War stories. The Korean War was barely over when Disneyland opened. Thousands of marines and other service people from the many Southern California military bases were among its early visitors.

The Vietnam War was still dividing the nation when Walt Disney World opened in 1971. I like to think the Magic Kingdom and Disneyland provided many thousands with escape from their military duties and a place to bring families closer together even if their views differed along generational lines.

Another example of a Disney World patriotic celebration that sparked a unique and surprising publicity event occurred in 1987 with the All-America Parade staged as part of the two hundredth anniversary of the U.S. Constitution. During our publicity build-up, I was telling Walter Cronkite about the upcoming parade, one of the largest we'd ever presented. I showed him artists' renderings of seventeen giant floats representing famous American landmarks. Cronkite told me his friend, Chief Justice Warren Burger, was looking for ways to get the public more excited about celebrating the Constitution's bicentennial.

"You ought to get together," he said.

Walter called the Chief Justice the next day. The result was a surprise press conference on the day the press arrived for the Grand Opening of the parade. We arranged to use the newly completed Orange County Convention Center's largest hall. When Justice Burger walked out on stage, the press seemed totally shocked to discover the Chief Justice joining his efforts with Disney. They rose and applauded. Burger spoke about the American dream that inspired our Constitution, a speech Walt certainly would have appreciated.

It was carried by television all across the country. I don't know who got the most publicity out of the unusual "partnership" with the Chief Justice. I know the Bicentennial got to be a truly national event and our parade was one of the most successful we ever staged.

Disney held many other patriotic events over the years, but none garnered more international attention than when President and Mrs. Ronald Reagan came to Epcot for the President's Second Inaugural Parade on May 27, 1985. The original parade, in January, had been cancelled because of cold and snow in Washington, D.C. Scores of marching bands from around the country were bitterly disappointed.

So Michael Eisner invited every last one of them to come to Florida to parade for the President and the First Lady. All of Orlando pitched in to cover the expenses and 2,500 bandsmen from sixteen states participated. The event made television news and newspaper headlines around the world. That sort of bold stroke was pure Eisner and the publicity was priceless.

Perhaps the happiest event of all was the dedication of *It's a Small World* when it was brought back to Disneyland from New York. For whatever reason, Walt seemed more relaxed and proud than I had ever seen him. We had arranged as a publicity stunt to have bottles of water shipped from Disney offices around the world in fancy vases, jugs and bottles.

Walt and the president of the sponsoring Bank of America poured the waters into the Seven Seaways. A children's choir from Long Beach sang, for the first time anywhere, I believe, a new song, "Let There Be Peace on Earth."

My wife and children rode with Jack Lindquist's wife Belle and her children in the first boat through the attraction. There really was peace on earth that day.

Chapter 12

*T*raveling to meet the press was a major part of our publicity efforts even before I came to Walt Disney World in 1969. Our new markets were far away, unlike at Disneyland where nearby Southern California was its dominant market. I continued Eddie Meck's go-see-'em policy even though it meant longer trips. My staff and I went regularly to all the major cities in the East to meet the press and deliver stories in person. Many times, we didn't give out the stories unless they asked. We just got to know our press contacts and talked about things going on at Disney World. If we worked it right, the editor came up with his own ideas for a story.

Especially in the winter, when days were dark and cold up north, editors were more than willing to talk about sunny Florida. Those contacts led to a massive turnout of newspeople for later events in Walt Disney World.

That plan to head north in cold weather caused its own travel problems. I made one trip to Philadelphia in mid-winter during a blizzard. I skidded out to the suburbs to visit WCAU-TV, the CBS affiliate. Our main contact was the weatherman named Herb, but he failed me that day. The snow kept coming down. All the station personnel decided to stay overnight to be sure to be there for the following morning — and I had to stay with them. There was plenty of time to make friends.

One of my top aides, Rod Madden, still a vital part of Walt Disney World publicity efforts, recalls that our contacts with TV weathermen paid off later when we started sending out short TV feature clips — visual handouts for use on their weather shows. When the weather up north was its most frigid, we prepared a short TV film (this was before the days of video tape) showing people basking in the warm Florida sunshine. One showed Donald Duck in a small boat on Bay Lake fishing. When he pulled his "fish" out of the water it turned out to be a fish shaped sign saying "Don't You Wish You Were Here, Herb?" The name on the fish was individualized for each weatherman. Willard Scott loved it!

We also contacted news directors, producers, radio newsmen, travel writers and feature assignment editors on newspapers in all major markets as well as magazine travel editors headquartered in New York, Washington, D.C. and Chicago.

Much of what was accomplished for many years, even today, depended on those early press contact trips.

Later I expanded my press visits to Europe. My first time abroad was a free trip. SAS Airlines had brought a group of Scandinavian travel writers to see our preview center before we opened in Florida. In return, the airline invited me three years later on an "Inaugural" flight from Helsinki to Stockholm. Since I was going, I decided to add press contact visits to London, Paris, Frankfurt and Copenhagen. Disney merchandising reps in those cities helped arrange meetings with key travel editors.

In the London office, publicist Cyril James told me why his co-workers were so willing to support me and any other Disney efforts. During World War II, Disney Studios was not making money, or any movies except for military training films. The studio was actually losing money at the time in their war work. Yet every week, a CARE package arrived in London from Walt and Roy, filled with staples and little luxuries unavailable in war-time England. Talk about creating loyalty!

That 1974 trip was the beginning of many lasting international friendships among travel writers, but perhaps better remembered by me for what happened during my first visit to Paris. Carrying a heavy briefcase full of press kits — I often felt like an anvil sales-man! — I developed a pain in my left leg so severe that I called the hotel doctor.

My hotel had been booked by our man in Paris, Armand Bigle. He was used to taking care of Walt and other studio execs for years. So, to my surprise, I found myself staying in a top floor suite at the George V, way above my station in life. I called asking if they had a house doctor to attend to a pulled muscle in my leg. They sent a nurse right up.

"Where is the man with the metal in his leg?" she asked. Some-thing lost in translation there. I explained it was a painful muscle in my leg.

She told me the doctor would be back soon. Thinking at George V prices it might cost more than my leg was worth, I suggested I might go to his office. Not possible.

Soon the doctor came and, when he discovered I was with Dis-ney, broke into smiles and started telling me about all the times he had treated Roy or Walt Disney during their frequent trips to the French capital. Something of a comedian, the doctor diagnosed my problem as a heel spur, too much walking on cobblestone streets.

"Go see your doctor when you get home," he said, "You proba-bly won't have to have an amputation."

The bill was $15.

While wrapping my leg with an Ace bandage, he fumbled. The elastic gauze unwound as it rolled across the floor.

"Oops," he said to his nurse, "we flunked the examination again."

One other memorable time when the health bug hit, I had been in Europe for two weeks in early 1982. My wife, Gretta, met me in Ge-neva. She was always a plus in meeting press people, who frequently seemed to like her better than me. Many times spouses joined us for lunch or dinner. The local Disney rep, Bob Pollard, suggested we also stop in Zurich because that's where most Swiss travel writers were.

We switched tickets for the umpteenth time and flew to Zurich where Bob had arranged a luncheon with the press at the Zum Storchen Hotel in the downtown area. On the short flight over I developed a sore throat.

Half way through my slide show presentation I had to give up. In fact, I almost fainted. Again we called the house doctor. He diagnosed pneumonia, gave me a penicillin shot and ordered me to bed. The hotel was completely full but had one room that was not quite finished being refurbished. Switch plates hadn't been replaced, the paint was still slightly wet, but otherwise it was just fine. They let me have it.

It turns out that, according to the guidebooks, this was the best room in the house — with a smashing view of the river and Zurich's most famous buildings. Since I had to rest a lot with no TV, the view made the wait bearable for the next five days. Zurich has been a favorite city of mine ever since.

That was also the trip I made unscheduled stops in Rome, Paris and London in connection with Disney President Donn Tatum's campaign to begin "selling" Epcot's World Showcase pavilions to European nations. Marketing Vice President Jack Lindquist phoned me in Zurich and enlisted my help in notifying the press in each city ahead of Donn's arrival while I was still recovering from my illness. We had dinners early because of my need for a lot of rest. We often arrived at a restaurant while the waiters were still having their own dinner. Well, they don't eat until nine in Rome.

U.S. Embassy officials helped set up visits for Tatum to talk with government cultural officials in each country about the forthcoming opportunity for them in Epcot's World Showcase. Without any knowledge of Italian, I hired a driver/translator to take me around to the newspapers, which were frequently in very old, run-down-looking squares.

I gave the driver a brief rundown of Epcot and World Showcase so he would understand a little of what I would tell each editor. Only one spoke English. And I am still not sure if what the translator told them was even close to what I said. Oh well, what can you do?

I shocked a Disney promotion man who had joined me in Rome when I laid my briefcase on an eighty-foot long table while we waited for an Embassy public relations officer to return. The dark walnut table was shined like a mirror to reflect the gold leaf carvings of the lavish U.S. Embassy conference room all around us.

"Hey, it's no good if you can't use it," was my reply.

Besides, it was a soft case, no scratches. Anyhow, that's the embassy whose peeling paint gave Claire Booth Luce lead poisoning.

Other embassy officials helped Donn Tatum explain World Showcase to top Italian cultural officials and at press conferences when he arrived a few days later. By that time I was in Paris.

Incidentally, I think I had a hand in calling those showcases in Epcot by the name of the country instead of using the country name as an adjective as was the practice at most World's Fairs. So instead of the *French pavilion* or the *Mexican pavilion*, people now say, "I am going to *France* for dinner" or "Let's go see the film in *Canada*." Makes it sound like you are traveling the world, doesn't it?

One of my major roles through the years was visualizing and setting up pictures for special events, groundbreakings, opening ceremonies and so forth. Arranging the photo just right was particularly hard for the Epcot groundbreaking ceremony in 1979, which took place in the middle of a virtual swamp.

Workmen cleared a path through the thick brush using pine straw to make it solid enough for busses which would carry photographers, reporters and special guests to the site. We set up a pair of giant cranes to suspend a glittering tinsel mock-up showing the outline of *Spaceship Earth* to be built on that site as the major icon of Epcot. It was like an eighteen story artistic sculpture with strands of gold creating the illusion of a geodesic dome.

Workers had cleared an area of shrubbery and erected bleachers for a hundred guests, but it wasn't easy to place cameramen in just the right position to photograph the 185-foot-high shape of *Space-*

ship Earth and still be able to get President Card Walker in the picture as he pushed the plunger setting off a ceremonial blast that marked the beginning of construction with a celebratory fireworks extravaganza. In the background, a gigantic dump truck, the biggest made by General Motors, tilted up and a big *Epcot, 1982* sign unfurled.

We managed to get the picture, but the show director never forgave me for making workmen move the speakers' platform six different times to get just the right angle.

Three years later, Epcot became a spectacular new kind of Disney land. It is hard today to imagine that swampy brushland was turned into a glittering future world of ultra modern architecture. The nearby swamp is now a beautiful clear Lagoon surrounded by architectural icons that house the pavilions of the eleven nations that comprise the World Showcase. Each night, a spectacular fireworks show, "Illuminations," is staged on World Showcase Lagoon. On clear nights, the geodesic globe of *Spaceship Earth* is reflected in its waters. It's a beautiful sight.

Chapter 13

The long-range effect of Disney parks on guests is legendary. It began at Disneyland and continues at all the others.

I think the best story I ever read about the spell cast by a Disney park was by one of my favorite travel writers, Horace Sutton. As I mentioned earlier, he was a syndicated columnist, Norman Cousins' executive editor at *Saturday Review* and a legendary journalist in the travel industry.

Horace brought his family to Disneyland soon after I began work. Fortunately for me, Eddie Meck assigned me to go with them for the day. We did everything. His seven-year-old son, Patrick, and ten-year-old daughter, Miranda, were full of smiles. Horace and his wife, Pat, were a little leery of the roller-coaster turns on the *Matterhorn Bobsleds*. The kids were dying to go. I took them and was their hero for years to come.

Sutton's story, which appeared in *Family Circle* months later, was not about Disneyland. It was about the effect that trip had on his family for months afterward. Paraphrasing Horace's insightful story:

"When I would come home tired at the end of a troubled day, Miranda was in tears because her teacher scolded her for not turning in her math homework, Patrick left his skates on the stairs, where I stumbled over them, and Pat was worn out from shopping. Someone would say, 'Let's talk about our day at Disneyland.' All the troubles were gone and we were lost in remembering."

Horace and I were close friends until his death a few years ago. He wrote many more stories about our parks, all with great feeling and all growing out of that first visit.

Another of my favorite writers was Stephen Birnbaum, who died the same year as Horace, also of cancer. Steve and his wife, Alex, were best friends of mine for many years. In addition to his magazine, *Diversion*, Birnbaum appeared regularly on *Good Morning America* and wrote some of the best guidebooks in the world. I followed his advice in Europe, South America and many other places.

Steve became the originator and editor of the Walt Disney World and Disneyland official guidebooks, thanks to a casual conversation we had over lunch one day.

"We really need someone, outside the company, to do a credible, unbiased guide to our resort," I mentioned in passing.

"I'll do it," he said.

It became the largest selling guide to anywhere for several years. In fact, I got in a little trouble with Horace Sutton, who asked, "Why didn't you tell me first?"

Getting to know talented writers, journalists, television news personalities, photographers and reporters of all kinds was the best part of my job. Because I grew up with newspeople, I always felt more comfortable with them.

Although we may not have seen each other more than once or twice a year I considered them real friends. And they were friends *mostly* because of the good times and adventures we shared in the Disney parks.

I discovered early on Disneyland's amazing ability to reverse preconceived notions of people, like me, who just didn't like "amusement parks."

Helen Markel, managing editor of *McCall's*, called me to say she and her husband, Jack Stuart of the *New York Times*, wanted to come and see the park but they only had one hour to spend at the most.

I told her they couldn't see much in an hour but we would try.

Five hours after the tour began, she confessed to me their time really wasn't limited. Her husband had wanted to come but she resisted. She finally agreed if the limit was one hour. Her office door was always open to me after that.

David Brinkley was another of my media favorites. He told me when I first visited his NBC office in Washington in 1969, the best times he ever had with his two boys were the ones they spent at Disneyland when the boys were ten or twelve years old. Because of David's busy schedule their times together when they were growing up were limited. Later he came down for the opening of Walt Disney World and did a great piece on the "new city" that Walt had created in Florida. It was still "Walt's creation" five years after his death.

"Others promised great new cities with monorails running through, sleek new buildings, comfortable surroundings and everything working," David said on camera with the Contemporary Hotel in the background. "But no one has done it — no one but Walt Disney."

David always had a greater insight than most.

I remember when British journalists arrived for the opening of Epcot they expected to find a new town. I purposely tried to name it Epcot Center so people would understand that it was not a city where people actually lived, but a center for displaying new ideas and old cultures. The name difference was too subtle for most. The British, whose own "new towns" were pretty much failures, were apparently expecting a Utopia where people rode on air cushions and smiled at each other constantly.

When they found that Epcot was an entertainment park with Disney adventures exploring the future and international cultures, they cried foul and wrote disappointed reviews. I've always thought, however, that Epcot achieved the spirit of Walt's vision of creating a greater understanding of today's world and getting people excited about the possibilities of the future.

❧

What was accomplished in terms of environment and beautiful surroundings in Walt Disney World as a whole makes it, as Walt dreamed, a place unlike any in the entire world. The difference becomes very apparent when I drive my visiting journalist friends down northern International Drive in Orlando with its clutter of shops and garish signs or along U.S. 192 where a jumble of tourist shops, restaurants and small hotels stretches for twenty miles. Then we turn down Buena Vista Drive past the Lake Buena Vista hotels and Downtown Disney shopping/dining/nighttime entertainment area and on to the Epcot Resort area and Disney's Animal Kingdom. It becomes clear, there's no other place like it.

Even closer to Walt's futuristic city ideas is the town of Celebration, which is separate from Walt Disney World and its visitors, but just a short drive away. Imagineers and Disneyland planners sought to develop it as an ideal city with traditional Southern residential architecture that's a lot more appealing to me than glass and aluminum-sided buildings.

It is a carefully planned and controlled environment. Some, who expected an urban Utopia, have been disappointed by the new city. But most who live there seem extraordinarily content. It's beautiful to see, with spectacular landscaping and garages hidden in alleys behind the houses and apartments to keep its streets clear and clean.

When Walt announced the Disney Florida Project in the 1965 press conference, he spoke of building two cities, one traditional and one futuristic. The EPCOT plan itself was not revealed until after his death in a film made by Walt. He wasn't around to explain in detail how it would work.

If he meant to have a city where tourists could come and tramp through homes and neighborhoods to see amazing new ways of living, then I don't see how it could have worked. I certainly would not have wanted to have such an open house every day in my home.

But what we did build — sometimes with very innovative experiments like the AVAC vacuum trash removal system, solar energy, the silent monorails, extensive conservation measures and new construction techniques — truly was in keeping with Walt Disney's dream for the future.

While Walt Disney World's "residents" are not permanent, remaining only for a day or a week, the new "World" does, I believe, create a magical environment where things are run with care, efficiency and unfailing hospitality, where buses are free to resort guests and run on time, where things are always clean and new looking, where amazing new ideas are everywhere if you are not too busy having fun to notice.

No, it is not covered by giant plastic domes to control the weather, as a *New York Times* writer once misinterpreted Walt's words. Trains do not run in subways to leave surface streets free for private vehicles. You run into water when you dig down ten feet in Florida. But to me it is a real living community providing pleasant surroundings for its fifty thousand cast members, the two hundred thousand guests who come here on a busy day and the one hundred thousand temporary citizens who sleep here every night. It really is an EPCOT. At its center, Epcot park — notice I didn't say theme park — is just one part of the "experimental city."

So I say to those first British writers who were disappointed in what they saw, "Take a better look. Your countrymen agree with me by the millions. They are among the most frequent non-American visitors."

In fact, I say with some sadness, they would rather come here than go to Disneyland Paris.

The Disney name was always a good entrée for a publicity guy like me in any country. Meeting and getting to know some of the great newspeople of our time was great fun, even more so, I think, because my contacts loved to talk about Disneyland or Walt Disney World.

Among my favorites was Tom Brokaw, who came with his daughters. We talked about it every time I went to his office in New York for years. Peter Jennings brought his family on vacation. I was always welcome in his office at ABC until his untimely death.

Walter Cronkite came frequently. He and his wife Betsy were among the early visiting press celebrities. Their first visit was particularly memorable. We had an evening cookout aboard a float boat in Bay Lake with just Walter and our wives for the whole evening. Later he brought his grandchildren on several occasions.

With my news media friends, I was always ready to hear about their writings and travels and they were willing to listen to me brag about all our new Disney stuff. Richard Corliss of *Time* and his wife, Mary, a designer for the Museum of Modern Art in New York, came almost every year, called and had me take them on a tour of new attractions.

Joan Lunden and her then fiancé came to visit even before her first marriage and children. I took them around and we became friends. She later became the anchor for numerous Disney television parades, partly because of that first meeting. It gave us a chance to meet at least annually. She always arranged for me to come see *Good Morning America* when I was in New York and is still one of my favorite people. Maybe she'll be back again soon with those new twins.

Walter Anderson, whose *Parade Magazine* has the largest circulation in the nation, was one editor who resisted my calls for several years, referring me to assistant editors. I had a friend who worked closely with Walter and knew I wanted to see him. One day while on one of my missionary trips to New York, my travel-writing friend Bill Ryan called and said, "Walter will see you at 3 o'clock for five minutes if you can make it." I cancelled two other appointments and dashed over. We talked for an hour about a whole range of topics but mostly about what a great trip he and his children made to Walt Disney World.

When we finished talking, he said, "You know, you are the first PR guy who ever sat in that chair." I walked out feeling ten feet tall. From then on he was a "best friend," frequently taking part in Disney seminar programs and youth award projects, which we sponsored in Florida. He was great with kids, encouraging reading and good citizenship, a passion with Walter.

It's nice to see that Walter has moved up to be chairman and CEO of *Parade*.

Lowell Thomas was another celebrated journalist who became a friend during the last years of his life. Several times he took me to meet his famous friends at the Explorers Club in New York, people like General William Westmoreland and General Douglas MacArthur's wife, Jean Marie.

Lowell first called me out of the blue one day in early 1971 — I don't even know where he got my name — and said he wanted to visit the Jungle River we were building in Florida. It was six months before we opened.

I apologized for the mess of construction as we climbed over mounds and through bushes to see the river taking shape. It was warm enough, even in February, to make him take off the big Stetson hat he always wore. Lowell was a special hero to me because my Dad used to talk about having met him when both were reporters in Chicago. I thought his book, *With Lawrence in Arabia*, which made Lawrence of Arabia famous, was one of the world's great adventure stories.

Lowell came back twice after the opening. Then in 1972, I got a call from Lowell's son, Lowell Jr., then lieutenant governor of Alaska.

"Mom and I want to have an eightieth birthday party for Dad at Disney World," he said. I agreed to help plan it.

The idea was to bring eighty of Lowell's best friends, like World War I Ace Eddie Rickenbacker, WWII's General Jimmy Doolittle, New York's Norman Vincent Peale and all the rest of the who's who for a day at Disney. They chartered a 707 and flew the group to Orlando, staying at the Contemporary Hotel for one night. We arranged a special "world" cruise aboard the paddlewheel steamer on Bay Lake and Seven Seas Lagoon with performers in national costumes of several countries at each dock around the lakes.

At the banquet that night, Lowell showed his home movies, things like Tom Dewey playing softball at Lowell's farm while a smiling Franklin D. Roosevelt looked on from his open touring car. Golf pro Patty Berg was shown dedicating Lowell's private golf course on the farm and so on. Lowell and his wife stayed for three more days, but moved over to the Polynesian Village, which was his favorite.

On one other occasion, I waited while Thomas talked to Art Linkletter's wife on the phone. They had been skiing the week before in Colorado. Lowell, then in his eighties, was just fine. Mrs. Linkletter had broken a leg.

Lowell and Walter Cronkite came to Orlando many times for an annual fund-raising banquet given by Henry Landwirth for his Give Kids The World Village. Walter and Henry were friends from the days when the Cronkites stayed in Henry's Starlite Motel while covering space shots at Cape Canaveral. Henry later moved operations to his Holiday Inn in Kissimmee.

Hundreds of children dying of cancer or other fatal diseases were brought to Walt Disney World for a final vacation with their families. They needed a place to stay, but our own hotels were booked up far in advance, often for years. Henry frequently provided rooms for these kids, but saw a need for more space.

So he built Give Kids The World Village, a unique place offering those families free transportation and lodging. Walt Disney World and other entertainment places provided tickets. The drawing power of Walt's world was so powerful that it was the last wish for thousands. They are still coming each year. Disney characters frequently go to have breakfast with the youngsters.

The Village offers meals, counseling and all kinds of special services for grieving families, many provided by corporate sponsorships as well as private donations. For many, it is the last time their family will ever be together. Henry told me that the stress of such illnesses frequently splits the family completely after the youngster's death. He sees his Village as repayment to this country, where he learned to live again after surviving five years as a child in a Nazi death camp during World War II.

People like Walter Cronkite and several of the astronauts help to keep the Village alive. After I told Walter Anderson about it, he arranged a major feature story in *Parade*.

Myrna Blyth, longtime editor of *Ladies' Home Journal*, was another of my favorite journalists who went on to national prominence among the country's top magazine editors. Myrna and husband Jeffrey Blyth came with their then pre-teenage sons in the 1970s and produced a great first-person account of their Disney experience for *Family Circle* magazine. It was the first of several family visits while the two boys were growing up and after Myrna moved to *LHJ*. "Those trips really were among the important moments in our lives for many years," Myrna says.

Jeffrey is a newspaper and radio correspondent for several British media. I called him recently for the first time in years. The first thing he said was, "Remember that elegant night at the Grand Floridian Opening when you provided tuxes for all the men? That was really something!"

Imagine a veteran journalist accustomed to hobnobbing with New York society remembering, with awe, when he was among five thousand guests who dressed in formal attire for a Disney World Resort opening twenty years ago. I'll have more to say about that unique event later.

Myrna's prime recollection was all the rainfall at several openings, particularly the night of the premiere of World Showcase when the Blyths were among thousands marching through the rain behind a one thousand piece band, with umbrellas bobbing in time to the music. "Everything was pretty dry but my feet," Myrna recalls. "My high-heel shoes completely disintegrated."

The family was also supplied with umbrellas for the showery Disney-MGM Studios opening in 1989 and the drizzly opening of

Splash Mountain in 1992, when the umbrellas were bright yellow instead of the black ones at other openings.

"We had a stack of Disney umbrellas around the house for years," Myrna reports. You can tell those were fond memories. Perhaps the rain helped make them special.

Ms. Blyth, who still writes for numerous publications, was recently named Chair of the President's Commission for the White House Fellows program, succeeding Julie Nixon Eisenhower. The commission selects outstanding young men and women for a year's experience working in executive offices at the White House, State Department and other special posts. Colin Powell was once one of the "fellows."

One journalist's visit gave me one of the most unusual evenings of my life. The head of United Press International in New York had been to China on a visit and in return took the chief UN correspondent for the Chinese News Agency for a tour of the East Coast. The UPI chief called me to help with arrangements for a stop at Walt Disney World. The Chinese correspondent arrived in his heavy wool Mao jacket on a hot fall day. As I took the two of them around, I couldn't see how he could stand the heat. Finally he gave in and went in shirtsleeves.

Knowing that Admiral Joe Fowler had served in the U.S. Navy in China, I arranged for him to host us for dinner in his cottage at Bay Hill, next door to the house we stayed in when I surveyed my new job years before.

Joe was always known as an exceptional host, a real gentleman. During the dinner conversation, Fowler and our Chinese guest discovered they must have faced each other across the Yangtze River when the Admiral was a young naval officer aboard a U.S. gunboat. The Chinese journalist was publishing his underground Communist newspaper carrying a printing press on the back of a donkey. Talk about the good old days!

One of my good contacts in the eighties was William F. Buckley, of public television and magazine fame, who made several tours of the park with me. He knew a lot of wealthy and important people, of course, and called me one day to ask a favor for a banker friend from Brussels, Belgium. He needed a reservation at the Grand Floridian Hotel — on Easter weekend no less! — and he wanted the Presidential Suite. Like always, everything for Easter had been booked many months in advance.

We pulled as many strings as possible and finally were able to get two rooms at the Grand Floridian on the concierge level. The price was about $850 per night for the two rooms.

I sent back word through Buckley that we had been able to find space. We didn't hear anything for two weeks. The weekend was getting near. My secretary called the banker's wife, a countess as I recall, who said they had made other arrangements.

"At that price, it can't possibly be up to our standard of luxury," she sniffed.

I should have known. I never did tell Buckley.

Another of my favorite media friends is ABC's Charlie Gibson. We haven't talked in a while, but we got to know each other long before he became the star of *Good Morning America*, He came on assignment during Gerald Ford's campaign to serve a second term. That tells you how long ago. Charlie was to do a piece on humor in American politics going way back in history, so he asked to film on stage at the *Hall of Presidents*, highlighting Abraham Lincoln and other past presidents known for their humor.

Such filming was dead against our standard policies. When seen from a distance, the way they were designed to be seen, those Audio-Animatronics presidents look almost too real to be human. The effect can be lost in close-ups. Charlie was so nice about it that I went to work and, after several calls to California, was able to clear the way. Charlie stood beside the presidents to tell his story.

Somehow the presidential race heated up so much that, as far as

I know, Charlie's humorous story never ran, but our friendship, however infrequent, was formed. I visited him on the *Good Morning America* set during annual visits to New York several times, always getting a cordial reception.

I would never try to prove that my visits resulted in publicity breaks for Disney, but they were a vital part of our efforts to encourage travel writers, editors, broadcasters, and journalists of all kinds to come and see our parks for themselves, the way Eddie Meck had taught me. And when they came to visit, we tried to spend some time with them and their families, making sure they had a good time. That was the most enjoyable part of the job.

The result was a long list of wonderful friendships, and Rod Madden and others who went to the electronic media with story ideas could always count on a friendly welcome.

Many of the meetings in newsrooms and editors' offices were spent listening to our media "friends" talk about what a great time they had the last time they visited. We never had to try to "sell a story" and many times never even left a news release. In the case of travel editors, who had the space for stories on Walt Disney World, we provided pictures and releases on new attractions and entertainment in the parks and hotels. Bigger papers always rewrote those press releases, but they frequently sparked ideas that resulted in major feature stories.

From our perspective, the best results came when writers thought up their own story ideas, or at least thought they had.

Chapter 14

$\mathcal{M}$ost of my world travels and many of my prized friendships resulted from my association with the Society of American Travel Writers (SATW), which manages to have its annual convention in far off places. Sharing those travels abroad brought me together with great editors and travel writers like Neil and Judith Morgan in San Diego; David Molyneaux and his writer wife, Judy Dash, in Cleveland; the late Kermit "Bus" Holt of the *Chicago Tribune*; and Don Carter, formerly a top editor with Knight-Ridder newspapers.

Holt was one who resisted Disneyland for years. Eddie Meck had been to see him every year and told him all he could about the park. Finally Holt came for the Tencennial. After a day in the park, he turned to Eddie and said, "Why didn't you tell me what this place was like?" I've heard the same question from other travel editors who came late.

My bosses understood the importance of our contacts, particularly with the travel media, but occasionally there were questions. For example, when Dick Nunis, then chairman of all Disney resorts, looked at my request for authorization to go to Bangkok for the SATW convention, he called in our marketing personnel director.

"What's Ridgway going to Thailand for?" he inquired with an edge in his voice. "How many Thais do you think we have among our visitors?"

My friend Tom had to explain I wasn't going to get publicity in Thailand. I was attending a meeting with some of the best travel writers in America. Since then I have made similar trips to conventions in Hungary, Brazil, Australia, Spain, and so forth. Since retirement I have maintained my associate membership in SATW, still talking with my old friends about Disney. The next meet is in Manchester, England.

In addition to media celebrities, I have had extraordinary opportunities over the years to rub shoulders with show business stars, international political leaders and other interesting folks. Although our Guest Relations and Special Affairs departments handled most of the arrangements for those celebrities, for some unknown reason some would call me instead.

Of all the celebrities, Helen Hayes was my favorite. We first met when she came to Disneyland for "Herbie Days," following the success of *Herbie Rides Again*, in which she appeared. We had a similar day at Walt Disney World years later. She would call when she was going through town and I would arrange a park tour or reserve a hotel room or whatever else was appropriate.

I remember one night standing in a suite on the fourteenth floor of the Contemporary Hotel. Looking out over the Seven Seas Lagoon and the lights shining from the Magic Kingdom, Helen said, "You know, I have been all over the world and I have looked down from the heights of Hong Kong and Oslo and many other wonderful places, but there is just nothing like this." I happen to agree.

Bob Hope was another celebrity who would call my office frequently when he was traveling our way. One day, he phoned saying he wanted to come tour the park the next day. "Great," I said, "we're opening a brand new parade and I'd like you to be our Grand Marshal."

No problem. He showed up on time, waved his way down Main Street in the electric surrey and made a hero out of me for arranging his appearance. I never told co-workers that it was all a coincidence.

❧

Parades were always a big deal in Disney parks, beginning with opening day at Disneyland, and they got bigger by the year. For the Magic Kingdom grand opening TV show in Florida in 1971, Entertainment Director Bob Jani assembled a whole passel of floats and a thousand-piece marching band from colleges and high schools all over the state. When they started marching out of tunnels on either side of the Main Street Railroad Station I thought the procession would never end. They filled the entire street. Five years later, at the opening of *Space Mountain*, the band grew to two thousand musicians and several astronauts were on hand to show off their new moon rover.

The parade I liked best was maybe the hallmark of my career, Donald Duck's Fiftieth Birthday Parade. I had absolutely nothing to do with the rest, but one element I will claim credit for is the fifty white Peking ducks we trained to follow Donald Duck down the street and to ride in the parade every day aboard a special float built just for them.

Months before in brainstorming sessions I wondered out loud, "Wouldn't it be fun if we could get fifty ducks to march down the street behind Donald — the one who greets guests each day in the Magic Kingdom?"

There was kind of an amused silence, more like disbelief. But someone said, "Do you think it can be done?"

We didn't know, but I called Charlie Cook, who was in charge of birds and such on Discovery Island. He had just trained a dove to fly on cue for a commercial. He didn't know about training ducks, so he called his veterinary friends.

"Yes," they said, "But you have to bond with them from birth."

So we arranged for Donald to be in the Miami hatchery when they broke out of their shells as fuzzy little yellow ducklings. The pictures of that event were great and ran on NBC news. We brought the ducks to Fort Wilderness Campground and every day Donald would go out to their little barnyard, throw out lettuce and get the ducks to follow.

As they grew larger and turned into white-feathered Pekings, we built a pen for them behind my office in City Hall. It seemed natural since they were going to a party to put little cone-shaped hats on them. And we added nametags pinned to velvet ribbons around their necks. There was Dopey Duck, Alice in Wonderland Duck, Big Bad Wolf Duck and forty-seven other Disney character names.

But there was a problem — in fact there were two. How to fasten the paper hats to the ducks' heads and how to keep them on. Gene Hawk (no relation to the predatory bird of the same name) came up with hats in many colors and a plan to fasten velcro to the duck's head feathers so it would not injure the ducks in any way. The hat could then be placed on the head or removed easily. It worked fine. But we discovered that when you put a hat on one duck the others immediately attacked in a jealous rage.

The solution? Put a divider in the pen. Put a hat on one. Put him on the other side. Add another and so on. As long as all the other ducks had their hats on, everything was fine.

Now what about a birthday cake? We tried all kinds of baked cakes. The ducks showed no interest. Ducks like corn. So why not freeze corn in circular pans and create a layered cake? They *loved* it.

For the grand opening, we had Clarence Nash, who provided Donald's voice for forty years, on hand to give the ducks a send off. Donald and Clarence marched off down the street. The ducks followed down to the castle where the cake was placed on an enclosed lawn off to one side.

The quackers nibbled at the cake for a while then decided to take off for the water in the Castle moat. Hot day. They didn't want to come out. Charlie Cook volunteered. He waded into the water and herded the ducks back so they could appear on their float later in the day.

Ducks, it appears, when they get warm or excited, pant — opening and closing their beaks to help them cool off. So when they came down the street aboard their float with quack-quack music playing, it looked like they were singing along.

People stared in disbelief. I stood by one woman when she

turned to her husband saying, "My God, Henry, look what's coming now!"

My reputation as a master of duck magic was secure.

The postscript came at the end of the year when the parade ended. We couldn't very well abandon our fifty charges or plan a big duck dinner. So we arranged to donate a pair of ducks to each of several zoos around the country and get a little publicity while we were at it. My former secretary, Louise Gerow, traveled with the Walt Disney World Ambassador to deliver the ducks. They came with party hats, name tags, and a certificate attesting to their authenticity as Donald's Ducks. Many became a top attraction at their zoos, including the Columbus Zoo where Jack Hanna of television fame accepted them.

You think that wasn't a fun job? People still ask about those ducks.

Speaking of proper names with meanings, like Gene Hawk's. One of my favorite Disney Imagineers, John Hench, continually reminded me that Mickey Mouse is not a Mouse, any more than Howard Green has a green face. Mouse is just Mickey's last name. Come to think about it, Mickey doesn't look like a mouse nowadays. John said Mickey is a personality. Mickey is Mickey and there is only one. Like Santa, he may be in many places, but you will never see two at the same time.

John was an Imagineer for nearly sixty-five years before his recent death. The Hench portrait of Mickey and Walt together is a classic. John never lost his affection for the little guy who started it all.

Many newspapers refuse to treat Disney characters as real personalities. They refer to "those actors who walk around the park in Disney costumes." But to us and the people who hug and kiss them and get their autographs, they are very much alive. And its not just kids who act that way. Watch Pluto hugging an eighty-year-old or dancing a jig with an Irish cop.

The people who play Disney characters in the parks are very protective of their identities. Although their job requires them not to talk about their roles, some are downright paranoid about it. The best Snow White I have ever known would never give her real name to anyone ever, not even me, while she was in costume. When in her own clothes she would never admit to her best friends that she was Snow White. She even refused to take part in a reunion of all the pretty girls who had played the part at Walt Disney World during our first twenty-five years.

That is something we would never have done with a character whose human face doesn't show. This particular Snow White had an amazing memory and would greet particular youngsters by name and a hug on their second or third meeting with her in the park, particularly those who traveled in wheel chairs.

All the characters were asked to maintain their on-stage identity while in the park and not discuss their jobs outside but not all of them were quite so determined as that Snow White.

We were frequently asked to let someone borrow a Mickey costume for a birthday party. No can do. In addition to everything else, we are talking about a $5,000 — at least! — piece of merchandise. That's pretty plush.

I will have to admit that my then four-year-old son, Scott, was more than a little surprised one day when he went into a backstage men's room. He came running out with a grin from ear to ear yelling, "I just saw Mickey Mouse in the toilet."

That seemed to be one of Scott's favorite subjects as a four-year-old. Shortly after I began work there, we took an aging Aunt Ida Belle to the park. Scott was our tour guide.

"Over there is the train station," he said, "There is the toy store and over by City Hall, that is the potty." Important things first!

My twenty-month-old daughter Janet's first visit was to ride King Arthur's Carousel. We had to stay busy while Mommy was having Scott. Later we used Janet, dressed like Alice in Wonderland, as a model for photographs. Every time I go, I see youngsters in the parks dressed like Cinderella or Snow White or Minnie Mouse. They are starry-eyed.

Even before I began working at Disneyland, my children celebrated birthdays by taking friends to the park. One time we visited the deck of the sailing ship *Columbia* after cake and ice cream. We were trying to keep track of ten little girls and boys. Only later did I discover in looking at pictures of the party that my son Scott and a friend had dangled precariously over the railing. Six adults at the party, including me, hadn't seen a thing.

When they were young, I frequently used my children or those of friends and coworkers as models for our photographs. We never thought of paying modeling fees in those days except for maybe a five-ride ticket book, but in today's Disney World photographers are required to hire and pay professional models for advertising and publicity shots.

Both of my children worked in the Walt Disney World Magic Kingdom when they reached age eighteen. Scott sold balloons and then worked in Fort Wilderness for a year driving trams and telling tall tales to guests. He invented tales of ghosts and giant snakes as the tram made its way along moonlit roadways in the wooded campground area. Weird sense of humor that boy. Janet worked at the *Frontierland Shootin' Gallery* and as a waitress on the *Mark Twain* steamboat. Later she interned one summer in the computer department.

Many children, husbands, wives and siblings, sometimes whole families worked in the park. It was encouraged. Who better to represent Disney than someone who had grown up with it?

Everyone, including Walt, was on a first name basis. He got upset if people called him Mr. Disney. Kids could get by with "Uncle Walt," but he was "Walt" to everyone else.

We carried the habit to outsiders as well. The reporters, editors and radio news celebrities who became my friends were always David, Walter, Tom or Peter. I heard Claire Booth Luce complain one time about people who started calling her by her first name without permission. She would not have done well in our parks.

Even in the diplomatic world, *first name* became a Disney trademark. In 1978, when we began selling participant sponsorships in Epcot's World Showcase, we invited Ambassadors from many nations for a weekend of presentations on the plan. About nineteen accepted and arrived in their dark suits and best behavior, despite the heat in Florida.

Immediately we encouraged them to take off their jackets. We pinned oval nametags on them with their first names, just like the ones cast members wear. They began dropping the "Mr. Ambassador" form of address and started calling each other by their first names. They probably never knew them before. By the time we took them to the *Hoop-Dee-Doo Musical Revue* two days later, they were regular fellas — completely different from the very proper diplomats who had arrived on Friday.

We managed to bring informality, but not much success, to selling government sponsorship of World Showcase pavilions, mostly because, while countries were prepared to back one-year sponsorship at World Fairs, they were unable to commit to a ten-year program that had to bridge multiple years of budgeting. And it wasn't inexpensive. Many of the ambassadors at the World Showcase meeting were helpful, however, in introducing Disney World to corporate sponsors who have played a role in financing some of the nations of Epcot.

When Walt was asked at the 1965 announcement of his plans for Florida how much he planned to spend, he replied, "Well, we have about $57 million invested at Disneyland now. I suppose it could go over $100 million." Walt Disney World cost $400 million to open six years later and it now represents billions of dollars invested. By 1978 we were used to spending a hundred million dollars or more on one major attraction. That might have made Walt wince.

Another major gathering of international leaders gave Disney officials a chance to tell them about World Showcase and demonstrate just what our Disney cast could do. It was the convention of the International Chamber of Commerce at the Walt Disney World Contemporary Hotel in 1978.

These were the oil barons, the top industrialists and financiers, two thousand of them from around the world. They chose the Disney site because of a sour experience in Madrid four years earlier when communist protesters yelled and demonstrated outside their hotel. Inside the circle of Disney magic they felt — and were — secure.

The highlight of the convention was a speech by President Jimmy Carter. At the time, there was no Disney convention hall big enough to hold all two thousand delegates, so we planned all the other events in sections, scattered among several venues. The gathering also gave us an opportunity to show off plans for World Showcase to important international leaders. We used two ballrooms linked by television for that so all could see. But for the main event they wanted all the delegates in one place.

So despite the too-good chance of October showers, the Carter address was planned in front of Cinderella Castle, a beautiful sight on a clear evening. Which brings me to another phenomenon that Patty Disney — Roy E. Disney's wife — called *Walt's Weather*.

Time after time — both before and after Walt's death — I have seen many important Disney events escape bad weather. Cloudbursts would suddenly stop and even all-day rains would break just long enough to let a parade or other outdoor show proceed unscathed.

I discovered Walt's Weather during my first year at Disneyland. To kick off the Christmas season's daily parades, the park staged a one-day super spectacular called the Parade of All Nations, inviting folk groups in colorful costumes from the ethnic communities in Southern California to compete for prizes. It had grown into a huge event with scores of marching bands, drum and bugle corps, dancers, prancers and horse-drawn wagons covered with colorful banners and smiling children.

The park was always overcrowded for the event, but that year it started raining early in the morning, sometimes a drizzle, sometimes a downpour. In fact it never stopped raining in downtown Los Angeles. The parade was scheduled for two o'clock. At 1:58 p.m. the rain stopped. The parade started and went on for a full hour. At 3:02 p.m., the rain started in again, but the parade was all done.

Walt's Weather turned up again at the Grand Opening of Walt Disney World in October of 1971, always a month of sudden showers in Florida. Events were spread over a two-day weekend. All of it was being taped for TV with stars like Julie Andrews, Glen Campbell, Jonathan Winters and Bob Hope.

During the preceding days it stormed every afternoon. But Saturday afternoon was sunny for Bob Hope's dedication of the Contemporary Hotel and Glen Campbell's song in Fort Wilderness. Thunderclouds were all around, but no rain.

The most glamorous of the planned events, however, was a black-tie concert in front of Cinderella Castle on Saturday night. We had gathered a World Symphony Orchestra made up of first chair players from around the world, under the baton of Arthur Fiedler. As the concert began, with guests seated all around the Castle, huge clouds began rolling in. Flashes of lightning and peals of thunder seemed to be keeping time with the tympani. It rained within a half mile of the park, but those clouds never squeezed a drop on our concert. The following day's parade of floats and a thousand-piece band played to sunny skies.

The International Chamber of Commerce event in 1978, however, was a different story. As President Carter delivered his relatively short address, thunder and lightning threatened. Our security department radar could see the storm approaching.

Since the party was private, we were able to waive the no liquor rule and plan a champagne party up and down Main Street following the address. As the President finished the last word of his speech and ducked into the Castle Keep, the first huge raindrops started falling. Suddenly two thousand umbrellas appeared as if by magic. (They had been stored in plastic rubbish cans all around the hub in front of the castle.). Every delegate had one in time to avoid the torrential gush that followed as they made their way up the street and into the Main Street shops, which were quickly opened for the party.

Some of the TV crews atop a twenty-foot platform were not quite so lucky as they carried large studio-size cameras down slippery ladders. Several cameras were drowned beyond repair. But the ICC delegates and the rest of the covering press stayed remarkably dry.

There was one problem, however. The champagne was stored and poured in large trucks parked just behind Main Street. So Disney cast members had to walk through the downpour carrying trays of goblets in to the sheltered delegates.

Women servers came into the shops with dripping hair and water streaming down their faces. Like the men, their costumes were soaked, but they had nothing but broad smiles and happy words for the ICC bigwigs. I don't know how diluted the champagne was, but no one complained.

For the next three days, all the business leaders talked about was the incredible performance of these smiling young Disneyites.

"If that had happened in Chicago, the unions would have stepped in, the waiters would have walked out and we would have been left stranded," they all agreed.

It was as if we had planned the whole thing just to impress the delegates. I don't remember hearing any comments about the Carter speech.

I still believe the spirit shown that night was somehow inspired by Walt himself, even though none of these young cast members ever saw Walt. Most were babies when Walt died. But they are as protective of the Disney legacy as any of us who knew him.

❧

There are other prime examples of Walt's Weather gone askew, the Grand Opening of the Epcot World Showcase in 1982 for one. The three-day event began under sunny skies with the landing of twin British Airways and Air France Concordes at Orlando International Airport and opening ceremonies at *Spaceship Earth*. The first night's semi-formal party opening Future World went well, too, a beautiful starlit night with music by Count Basie's Band and other top entertainers playing under *Spaceship Earth* and in *CommuniCore* (a centrally located display area since used to house *Innoventions*). I remember riding *Spaceship Earth* with author Alex Haley and later with Hollywood columnist Marilyn Beck.

But the next day, World Showcase Day, dawned gray and threatening. It started drizzling, which in Florida means you're in for a long day. Heavy showers usually end soon, but not drizzle. We had brought folk dancers, bands and horn ensembles, stilt walkers and international entertainment of all kinds from twenty-six countries around the world.

They had to be moved indoors to makeshift venues all around World Showcase. I remember being amazed at Czechoslovakian dancers flying through the air above the hard, hard marble of the rotunda floor in the *American Adventure* (now renamed the U.S.A. pavilion). The rain let up occasionally, giving some hope. The Canadian Mounted Police horses were able to march elegantly around the circle of the showcase. The Belgian Hunting Horns played and the Yugoslavian stilt walkers were even able to perform briefly between showers.

The ten thousand VIP guests, including hundreds of press from many nations, were able to tour the nations — Mexico, China, Germany, Italy, American Adventure, France, United Kingdom and Canada — to sample food and see dramatic films. Again, thousands of umbrellas handed out early in the day kept guests reasonably dry.

Our grand parade with a thousand-piece marching band was to climax the evening at nine. At 8:30, the rain subsided. Walt was watching after all. Let the parade begin.

Just as it did, the downpour resumed. I remember seeing the beater sink deep into the side of the bass drum, producing nothing but a "squish," but the horns played on and led the way. Thousands of guests followed, holding their black umbrellas high and pumping them up and down in time to the music. What a sight!

When they reached *CommuniCore*, the marching crowd was directed through covered hallways arching around either side. Inside were smiling but still wet hosts and hostesses bidding a Disney farewell.

Years later my media friends remembered that night above everything else they saw during the opening.

The final day of the Grand Opening was also outdoors in front of *Spaceship Earth*. The U.S. Army's West Point Glee Club sang, Danny Kaye entertained, and folk groups from all the nations finally got a chance to parade outdoors for our guests. The day was chilly enough to hand out thousands of blankets. The skies were overcast but there was no rain. Walt's Weather won after all.

Getting ready for World Showcase produced another humorous highlight for me. The park hired a social behavior guru from Washington, D.C., the wife of a New Orleans correspondent, to come down and teach us the finer points of international social behavior. With her thick southern accent, the very proper madame showed us which fork to use for shrimp, how to debone fish, and how to hold our napkins. She even taught how to behave if someone has a heart attack during a banquet — stay still and let the people at the stricken person's table drag him out.

I finally could keep my weird sense of humor in check no longer. We were instructed to give our names to the maitre d' so we could be announced to the receiving line. I told him to announce my wife and me as Pope John and Mrs. Paul. Okay, so I am naturally uncouth. My wife frowned. My left ankle still gets sore in wet weather.

I can't recall we ever had to use any of that training, although maybe it was because I just wasn't invited. I did dine one night with the Empress of Iran at the Empress Lilly riverboat restaurant, if that counts, and one other time with Michael and Jane Eisner and several important guests during a press event in 1994 or '95.

We were upstairs in Les Chefs de France. Three famous French chefs had agreed — surprisingly — to join forces and operate the fine restaurant in the France Showcase. All three Chefs de France — Paul Bocuse, Gaston LeNotre and Roger Verge, wearing their tallest toques — appeared to tell us they had planned a very special dinner for the group. With great flourish they personally presented the appetizer and later the dessert. We all thanked them for a great meal.

As we walked along beside French windows outside the dining room of their restaurant below after dinner, Jane and I both glanced in the window and burst out laughing. A hundred or so of our press guests were dining on exactly the same menu we had been served with such flourish.

All of which proves, I guess, that everyone is a VIP in a Disney park.

Chapter 15

The year 1989 was filled with enough special openings to keep our publicity and marketing team running like scared rabbits for the entire year. There was Typhoon Lagoon, Pleasure Island, and *Wonders of Life* (in Epcot), but as Ed Sullivan would say, the really big show was the opening of the Disney-MGM Studios.

Stars on hand for the May opening of the Studios park included Pee Wee Herman, Dick Van Dyke, Bryant Gumble, Jim Henson, George Lucas, Harvey Korman, John Ritter, Pat Boone, McLean Stevenson, Phyllis Diller and many more.

Walt's Weather played a part in that opening, too. During the cloudless morning, we had implanted the handprints of our many Hollywood guest stars in the sidewalk in front of our version of Grauman's Chinese Theater. Inside the theater, *The Great Movie Ride* depicted full-scale scenes from many famous movies, including *Singin' in the Rain*. Okay, keep it inside.

With thousands of press guests on hand, the main event was a nighttime "typical Hollywood premiere," set to begin with a parade of limousines arriving at the front entrance at seven in the evening.

In the limos were people like Kevin Costner, Bette Midler, Betty White, Buffalo Bob Smith, Steve Allen, Jayne Meadows and Walt's old friend, Art Linkletter, plus many more. Television cameras and klieg lights were positioned all along the street and roof-tops to tape the opening special. My longtime friend, Hollywood columnist Army Archerd, agreed to introduce the stars out front on a red carpet stage as he had at many premieres.

At three o'clock, it began raining heavily. It could have been disaster. Umbrellas couldn't have helped this time. It poured.

With five minutes to spare — 6:55 p.m. to be precise — the rain suddenly stopped.

Broom wielders pushed away puddles. The stars were loaded into their limousines behind the scenes. Lights, camera, action! But no lights.

The downpour had drowned cable connections so that scores of giant spotlights for the TV taping wouldn't come on. Electricians pulled out their hair dryers and went to work.

So while Michael Eisner and Jeffrey Katzenberg, then Chairman of Walt Disney Studios, walked up and down the row of limos for a solid hour, trying to keep impatient stars from bolting, everything was on hold. The excited crowd of invited "movie fans" and press waited, almost patiently.

Finally, after an hour, they threw the switch. The lights were on and so was the show. The rest of the evening was magically starlit. Willie Nelson, the Pointer Sisters and other name groups performed on separate stages.

And for the finale, hundreds of dancers in bright yellow raincoats and umbrellas pranced up and down Hollywood Boulevard in front of the Chinese Theater to the music of "Singin' in the Rain." But, thank Walt, there was no rain.

As a special part of the three-day Studios event, we created a salute to old-time television with a stage that looked like a 1950s television set. On stage for ceremonies and press interviews were people like Art Linkletter, Rose Marie, Dick Van Dyke, Buffalo Bob Smith and Betty White.

Having Hollywood celebrities around had always been important for major openings, but it was essential for establishing the credibility of Disney-MGM Studios as a working film factory and entertainment park where stars might be seen during any visit. After the initial rush to see the new park, attendance that fall needed help.

Remembering what Eddie Meck had told me of the long-range impact of having big name stars appearing at Disneyland — people like Peggy Lee, Benny Goodman, Louis Armstrong — so that guests could go home bragging about seeing stars, I suggested some kind of program that would bring stars to Disney-MGM Studios on a regular basis, not necessarily to perform but to be seen.

Tom Elrod, by then vice-president of marketing, expanded the idea and with the help of the Entertainment Division came up with an affordable plan called "Star Today."

Each week, a new star was invited to Walt Disney World for a vacation with his or her family. Without requiring full-scale performance fees, the stars were willing to appear in a daily parade down Hollywood Boulevard with Mickey Mouse in a bright pink Cadillac and do an hour's interview session on a stage next to the Brown Derby restaurant. There, seated on benches in front of the stage, two to three hundred adoring fans could ask questions they had always longed to ask their favorite stars.

Instead of the sort of probing questions celebrities usually get from the Hollywood press corps, the inquiries involved personal tastes, favorite colors, how they got into show business and that sort of thing. Seldom were they asked embarrassing questions about their personal lives. Movie stars, who seldom had a controlled opportunity to just chat with their fans, obviously enjoyed the sessions and frequently told humorous stories about their personal lives. I particularly remember when Andy Griffith appeared. His down-home approach was a big hit with the fans that day.

While only a small percentage of the people in the park each day took part in the question-and-answer sessions, thousands more could go home bragging about the star they saw, like Andy Griffith, Drew Carey, Angela Lansbury, Julie Andrews, Beau Bridges, Britney Spears, Michael J. Fox, or one of the many others who appeared at Disney-MGM Studios. The new park's reputation and attendance grew steadily. Other than a small ad in the *Orlando Sentinel* and internal publications distributed to guests, we never tried to publicize those appearances, but it was good publicity nevertheless.

Michael Eisner's vision of the Studios as an important and popular addition to Walt Disney World's entertainment menu proved to be one of the best of his early decisions.

For Jack Lindquist, Disney-MGM Studios was a throwback to his own youth growing up in Hollywood. He believes its re-creation of Hollywood Boulevard, circa 1930, created for today's generation of grandparents the same kind of magic when it opened in 1989 as Disneyland's Main Street, U.S.A., circa 1900, did for an earlier generation when it opened at Disneyland in 1955.

The old folks who came to Disneyland in the beginning could still remember and relate to their grandchildren the days when horse-drawn streetcars and gaslights were a part of everyday life. By 1989, hardly anyone still alive could remember those days. But the sixty-year-olds could remember how glamorous Hollywood Boulevard and the Chinese Theater were in the 1930s. By 1989, of course, California's Hollywood Boulevard had lost much of its glamour. The stars had all moved to Bel-Air or Malibu. NBC had moved from Vine Street to Burbank, CBS had moved to TV City on Beverly Boulevard and the Brown Derby was fading fast.

So Walt Disney World's Hollywood Boulevard helped to recapture a by-gone glamorous era much as Main Street, U.S.A. did thirty-five years earlier. Of course, we added to its glamour by putting the hand prints of all the stars who visited into the cement walks in front of our Chinese Theater, a tradition Sid Grauman had started in Hollywood fifty years earlier. Nostalgia always strikes a cord with people.

Most of our events were pretty informal but one was the exception — the Grand Opening for the Grand Floridian Hotel and Beach Resort in 1988.

Burt Reynolds and Loni Anderson were there in the morning to cut the ribbon with appropriate Hollywood glamour. It was the first big hotel opening after Michael Eisner and Frank Wells joined the company. Their first big decision was to give a go-ahead to construction of the hotel, which is as elegant as they come. It reminds people of the grand Victorian hotels of the nineteenth century, only brighter and prettier.

The main nighttime event was indoors. For the occasion we decided everyone should wear tuxes. We rented twenty-five hundred of them for the male half of our five thousand guests, including press. Getting all the men fitted with proper sizes was a real task. I'm glad others handled that. The women in the crowd had to come up with their own formals. Discrimination? Maybe, but none of the ladies complained.

At the magic hour that evening, we gathered in the spectacular atrium of the new hotel, arrayed around balconies on all five floors above the crowded lobby, and raised champagne glasses to toast the occasion. Several NASA astronauts were on stage for the salute along with Michael, Frank and other dignitaries. I was on the top balcony with tears in my eyes. Emotion will out at times.

It was another of those occasions when scores of guests commented, "No one does it like Disney." Don't tell me people don't think that Walt is still responsible.

The Grand Floridian was the first of many unique themed hotels created during the Eisner era in America and France. I watched them all grow, climbed construction stairs and led press tours. Many of them are not comparable to any others I know. Michael undertook an extraordinary program to enlist the services of some of the nation's best-known architects.

Working with Imagineer master planner Wing Chao, who holds a master's degree from the Harvard School of Design, he held competitions to select designs for each hotel, beginning with the most unusual Swan and Dolphin hotels, the wonderful Wilderness

Lodge, and including five unique hostelries in Paris. The Grand Californian at Disneyland is among the most recent of those celebrity architect creations and one of the best.

Besides the Grand Floridian, Michael and Frank faced another major hotel decision after taking over in 1984. A twin-hotel convention center was planned near other Lake Buena Vista hotels on the eastern edge of the property. Contracts had already been agreed on with Tishman Realty Co. The new leaders began negotiations to expand the project and move it the to the center of the property, near Epcot, and chose famous architect Michael Graves to do both interior and exterior design. The result was somewhat controversial because giant swan and dolphin statues atop the Swan and Dolphin hotels could be seen from inside of Epcot's World Showcase.

Because I am old fashioned I prefer designs like the Grand Floridian or BoardWalk hotels but I don't think the few glimpses from inside Epcot are a big deal. As major convention hotels, the Swan and Dolphin have many other attributes far more important — access, good operation, pleasant rooms, and real style and high visibility in the heart of the action.

My own favorites are the work of Robert A.M. Stern and Peter Dominick.

Stern's hotels recall the compelling architecture of the past, as Walt did with the Magic Kingdom. His work includes three hotels near the Swan and Dolphin in the Epcot Resort Area — the Yacht Club, the Beach Club, and the BoardWalk Inn — plus the Newport Bay Club and Hotel Cheyenne (Wild West) at Disneyland Paris.

Dominick's terrific work includes the Adirondacks-style Wilderness Lodge, with an atrium lobby that looks like Yellowstone's Old Faithful Lodge but many times bigger, and the tremendous Grand Californian in Anaheim done in a kind of rustic Frank Lloyd Wright style to harmonize with the adjacent Grizzly Mountain area of Disney's California Adventure park.

My favorite of all is the Victorian-style Disneyland Hotel designed by Disney Imagineering's own architects and the firm that designed the Grand Floridian. The one at Disneyland Paris bridges the entrance to its Magic Kingdom, taking its inspiration from Main Street, U.S.A. right outside its French windows.

That Victorian style hotel is now the inspiration for a new Disneyland Hotel at Tokyo Disneyland. Begun in 2006, it is scheduled to open in two years.

Michael became so well known for his interest in architecture that he was invited to meet with Britain's Prince Charles, who shared his passion. The two met at Balmoral Castle six months before the opening of Disneyland Paris.

To meet the needs of the broadest possible range of Disney guests, the luxury hotel additions were developed in tandem with middle- and low-end hotels such as the Coronado Springs, the Caribbean Beach, Dixie Landings, All-Star and new Pop Century hotels.

Also part of Michael's adventures with high-profile architects are the spectacular Team Disney buildings in Burbank and Florida. And there is the town of Celebration, with its many unique office and civic buildings by world-class architects.

At least a part of the experimental city that Walt talked about is a reality in Celebration and in the kind of dynamic new buildings added in the last fifteen years, not only in Florida but in France, California and Hong Kong, not to mention the restoration of the El Capitan Theater in Hollywood and the New Amsterdam Theatre and other projects in Manhattan.

The massive construction program instituted by the Eisner-Wells team was not limited to hotels and parks. Themed water parks were another form of entertainment pioneered and pushed to the limit by Disney. Our first such park had been River Country, a kind of Tom Sawyer swimming hole built mainly for Fort Wilderness guests, which opened in 1976. President Ford's daughter, Susan, came down to preside at the Grand Opening. How can you top that for a publicity break?

The idea came from several Imagineers who had grown up in Southern California and remembered sliding down waterfalls and rocky streams in the foothills above Pasadena. They designed slides in a series of cascading pools to look like rocky mountain streams where guests could bounce along in inner tubes. Waterfalls flowing into a heated swimming pool provided thrills as swimmers plunged from a pool above the falls straight into the main pool. A small lake was created as well as a flume ride that looked like it was made for transporting logs, but which sent swimmers twisting and turning down the flume to a splashing finale. It was all surrounded by dense woods and tall trees and was an immediate hit with young and old.

My own children were just the right teen age to enjoy it. Again, we used them as models for publicity photos. Still no modeling fees. They had too much fun to worry about that.

River Country was overcrowded, so one of Michael Eisner's first projects was to add Typhoon Lagoon, featuring a shark pool and a wave machine. As with all Disney attractions, the making of Typhoon Lagoon began with a story, a once-upon-a-time fable. In simplified form, the story in this case was: *A tropical island with a volcano was hit by a typhoon which twisted native buildings into weird shapes, left a little steam-launch teetering on the edge of the volcano and created a new playground for the kids.*

Every few minutes the volcano threatens to erupt, causing steam to rise and the boat whistle to blow. That is the signal for another wave, big enough for surf boarding, to roll across the lagoon at the base of the volcano.

The new attraction was especially appealing to the president of Disney parks, Dick Nunis. When the Seven Seas Lagoon first opened in 1971, Dick proposed building a wave machine that would let guests surf near the Polynesian Village Resort. Imagineers built huge hydraulic flaps to churn up the waves and experimented for many months. It never worked.

But they made it happen in Typhoon Lagoon, building a huge elevated tank hidden inside the volcano with valves that open on cue, sending a rush of water plunging down, creating waves four feet high. High-speed water slides send swimmers cascading down the mountainside. The Lagoon attracted special attention from surfing and water sports magazines. Typhoon Lagoon also features a shark pool where guests can swim with friendly sharks, a lazy river for rubber rafting, and typhoon-battered buildings to house changing rooms, merchandise shops, rental stalls and restroom facilities.

A few years later, when Typhoon Lagoon became overcrowded, Blizzard Beach was added with a kind of reverse sun country theme — a snow-slide ski mountain where water and painted rocks replaced snow and ice.

Under Michael Eisner, a small shopping village, mainly selling to employees in 1975, evolved into the vast daytime shopping and nighttime dining and entertainment complex called Downtown Disney. Part of Eisner's initial expansion effort was what came to be called Pleasure Island, an unusual complex of restaurants, shops and a half dozen nightclubs located beside a small creek in the Lake Buena Vista area on the eastern side of the property.

Imagineers invented a legend to explain the weather-beaten look of the "ancient waterfront warehouse area." I'm not sure many guests really demanded an explanation, but it gave the Imagineers a story to help them imagine and construct such a fantasy.

According to legend, *an eccentric inventor named Merriweather Pleasure built warehouses on the island for his somewhat weird experiments, including a ship building works and a fireworks factory. In days when there were waterways connecting the Island with the Atlantic Ocean, Merriweather's wealthy friends came to visit in palatial yachts. One night Pleasure's experiments with fireworks caused a giant explosion. Merriweather disappeared. The whole place was abandoned and fell into disrepair until Merriweather's heirs took over the warehouses and turned them into unique restaurants and nightclubs.*

So Pleasure's fireworks factory became a barbecue restaurant. The millionaire's yacht harbor became the Portobello Yacht Club

restaurant, and a nightclub called Mannequins Dance Palace offered disco dancers a glitzy atmosphere, flashing lights and contemporary dance music in a barn-like building. Another "old" store-
house was turned into the Comedy Warehouse. There was also a
three-story rock 'n' roll dance hall with a roller rink on the upper
level, a country music show and a jazz club nearby. Of course, all of
this was built from scratch.

Pleasure Island became a gated area with its own ticketing and
ID bracelets to identify those old enough to enter the places that
served liquor. The Island became a big hit by adding a nightly "New
Year's Eve Party and fireworks." In 1996 the spectacular ball-shaped
Planet Hollywood restaurant was added next to the Island. A new
section featuring yet more entertainment and shopping was added
later to the west of the Island and the whole area was renamed
Downtown Disney.

The West Side of Downtown Disney opened in 1998 and '99
featuring Cirque du Soleil, Virgin Records, House of Blues, Wolf-
gang Puck's restaurant and DisneyQuest, an interactive fun center.
Innovation in entertainment and architecture created a unique area
satisfying a long-time need for a bright nightspot for Walt Disney
World guests.

Just across the Reedy Creek waterway from Downtown Disney, a
new hotel complex has been added. Named Saratoga Springs Resort, it replaces earlier town houses that were originally designed as
condominiums but always used as nightly rentals.

That was also the area where Michael attempted a Chautauqua-
style education and entertainment resort with courses teaching everything from gourmet cooking to gardening and animation. The
Disney Institute, as it was called, was never quite able to compete
with the Disney park adventures for vacationers' time. I think it's
interesting that the area now takes on the character of Saratoga,
New York, where Chautauqua originated.

Like Walt, Michael was trying to combine education and entertainment. Although many of Disney's films, particularly the True Life Adventure Series, won awards for their educational content, Walt always said he would rather entertain first and if people learned something, fine. But not the other way around.

I think Michael had the same idea.

While new parks and attractions were being added, outdoor recreation facilities continued to grow — swimming, boating, jogging trails, fishing, tennis and especially golf.

Walt Disney World had barely opened in 1971 when our publicity department had to get ready to run the press tent for the Walt Disney World PGA golf tournament on the only two courses completed by that fall.

For the first twenty years, one of my jobs was to lead Mickey Mouse and friends onto the eighteenth green for the presentation of a trophy too big for Mickey to hold by himself. The first three years Jack Nicklaus ran away with it. Then we switched to a team format for a few years and Jack stopped coming.

But many other top pros came as the tourney grew into a Classic and a finale for the Tournament Players Division of the PGA each year. In many ways, it was a Cinderella tournament, with the trophy going to a first-time winner who went on to greater fame in later years.

Many of the players were encouraged to come by their families, who wanted a chance for a Walt Disney World vacation. The Magic Kingdom proved to be something of a distraction as kids would beg their golfing dad to take them to the park after the day's play, at least until the final rounds.

But for the average visitor, particularly during the early years, golf played second fiddle to the other entertainment. Attendance at the tournament depended on leading corporations and businessmen around the country who joined the Disney Golf Classic Club, which became very successful after the first year or so. The corporate sponsors distributed tickets among employees, customers, and business friends. Frequently the tournaments have been televised, providing exposure for the golf courses, the parks and the resort as a whole.

During the early years, we would use the company plane to fly local TV sportscasters to an earlier tournament to do interviews with pros scheduled to play in the Disney event. It did help attendance. The only casualty was one sportscaster who left his false teeth in the men's room when we went to North Carolina's Pinehurst Resort.

With the Magnolia and Palm courses in the beginning, a third course, Lake Buena Vista, was completed and added to the tournament in 1972. A year later, the Golf Resort Hotel with two hundred rooms was added. Years later it became Shades of Green and was taken over by Armed Forces Recreation for the use of retired and active military personnel. But we continue to operate the courses ourselves.

When Michael Eisner came aboard he hired two of the nation's premier golf course architects to design the Osprey Ridge and Eagle Pines courses on Bonnet Creek, near the eastern edge of the Disney property, making a total of ninety-nine holes of golf. Still another Disney course was designed for the City of Celebration by Robert Trent Jones Senior and Junior. I made good use of all those courses and still do. But despite a lot of publicity effort and having six of the nation's best courses, Disney World is still known more for its parks than its golf.

Chapter 16

The last big Walt Disney World addition I worked on was Disney's Animal Kingdom. I had a ball writing the Press Book for it because it gave me a chance hear fascinating stories from Imagineers who had been traveling to animal habitats around the world gathering designs and inspiration. Rick Barongi from the San Diego Zoo came to help assemble animals, mainly acquired from U.S. zoological parks. He told me of exciting adventures when he went to Kenya and the Masai Mara after leaving college.

Joe Rohde, a really flamboyant character, headed the Imagineering design team. He told me funny stories about bouts with monkeys in Bali or riding elephants in Nepal. He lived for several weeks among natives in the Himalayan back country far beyond any auto roads and became a hero by painting a portrait of the mayor of the village on a huge boulder.

Landscaper Paul Comstock told great yarns about letting his favorite elephant use her trunk to collect grasses and plants for seeds that would be brought back for planting in Disney's Animal Kingdom.

For three months, I accompanied our photographers in a van with a pop-up lid to photograph zebras, hippos, elephants, impalas, ostriches, giraffes, lions, rhinos and warthogs that had been brought in to inhabit our newly created African safari lands.

The Press Book stories so inspired me that three years later, I made a month-long trip to South Africa, visited nine game preserves including the gigantic Kruger Park, shot three thousand photographs of my own, and discovered Disney had duplicated the safari experience down to the last cat's paw. I got new cameras for my trip and practiced for the game preserves by shooting pictures at Disney's Animal Kingdom. I guess I'll have to go to India now to see if those tigers are as awesome as the ones in our Florida park.

Disney's Animal Kingdom Press Book and the ones I did for Walt Disney World's twenty-fifth anniversary and for the opening of Disney's California Adventure in Anaheim helped interviewers start their conversations with our people without having to ask who they were and what they did. I wish I had thought of it sooner.

I don't know what Walt would have said about the Animal Kingdom. He loved animals, of course, and did one of his best True-Life Adventure films on African lions. But when he built the *Jungle Cruise* with animals activated by Audio-Animatronics, he said its great advantage was having animals that would appear and perform on cue every six and a half minutes. That's tough to do with live animals.

The only fault I find with the entertainment provided by wild animals, either at Disney or in Africa is that, like fishing, you sometimes have to wait around quite a while before you get a bite. But Disney's savannah and the animals on it look so much like what I saw in Africa that I was really surprised.

Seeing this new animal park reminded me of following Walt Disney around twenty-five years earlier taking photographs while inspecting the new *Jungle Cruise* Audio-Animatronics animal figures during a major rehab. Many new animals and more sophisticated animation technologies were being added. He was like a boy with a new toy. Me too.

Like Walt, Roy O. Disney was very good with press people, as is his son, who in later years got to looking more like Walt than anyone I ever knew. I got to know Roy E. and his wife Patty during the building and opening of Disneyland Paris. Her dad was a famous

Hollywood correspondent for the *Saturday Evening Post* so we had something in common.

Partly because of Patty's Irish heritage and a brother who was former U.S. Ambassador to Eire, the Disneys have a castle in Ireland and came to France frequently. On opening day of Disneyland Paris, we arranged to have Michael Eisner and Roy, who had played a vital role in bringing Michael and Frank into the company, walk down Main Street with photographers ahead and all around them, "introducing the new park."

I forgot that most of those French, German and Italian photogs didn't speak English. They crowded around so closely, despite a handful of Disney security people with us, that I really became frightened for the safety of Michael and Roy. It is a wonder they didn't suffocate.

I think they were a little frightened too. My repeated, "Please move back, give us a little room," was either not understood or totally ignored.

All Michael ever said was, "Let's don't try that again."

This was one of many times when one of my jobs was arranging photo setups for openings and special events to produce the best pictures. Entertainment show directors had a habit of putting the key ceremonies and dignitaries too close to the front of the castle or the new attraction, resulting in photographs with nothing more than a gray wall in the background. I convinced them to move them out away from the building so the dignitaries were big in the foreground but the whole building was visible behind.

I usually managed to get out of the shot before cameras started clicking. But one time at least, I got caught while arranging Snow White and the Seven Dwarfs. Before I could get out of the way, our Disneyland Paris photographers started shooting. With mischievous intent, my friend Duncan Wardle in our London office managed to place it on the cover of an important British Sunday magazine. There I am peering out between Sneezy and Dopey. I forgot to whistle.

The opening in Paris, in keeping with the scope of the project, was a huge affair with celebrities and performing groups from all over Europe. We brought hundreds of press from all parts of France, Germany, England, Italy and Spain, Belgium, the Netherlands and Scandinavia, all considered vital markets. As usual, we provided accommodations, park access and other assistance. We traditionally provide tickets to the parks for reporters from recognized legitimate news organizations, a way of encouraging them to see for themselves what we have to offer.

We always made it clear that the passes and parties we staged were free of any obligation. When a writer said, "I'll do a story if you get me in," we always replied, "No, we don't make trades. If you see a story you think is good for your readers or viewers, do it; if not, don't do it."

The debate within the media over "freebies" was particularly hot in the 1970s. First came Mike Wallace and *60 Minutes* doing a story growing out of discussions at the annual Radio and Television News Directors Association (RTNDA) convention.

They interviewed several members at the convention, but before running the story decided to add other elements, including coverage of one of our press events, the premiere of the Disney animated film *Robin Hood* which was being held in Walt Disney World's Fort Wilderness. At the same time we were inaugurating service on the narrow gauge Fort Wilderness Railroad.

Mike's producer called saying they felt this was a "newsworthy event." Alerted by friends among newsmen who had become aware of the *60 Minutes* RTNDA interviews, we knew their true purpose was to "expose" our press guests as freeloaders. We agreed they could film the event as long as they did not interfere with our guests.

They asked to interview a Disney executive. Jack Lindquist, bless his heart, answered the call.

"Don't you think there is something unethical about hosting these press?" Mike asked.

"I don't know, Mike," was Jack's quick reply, "What do you think?"

It stopped the interview cold and exposed a certain amount of prejudgment on the part of *60 Minutes*.

The issue came up again a few months later at the 1973 convention of the Associated Press Managing Editors in Disney's Contemporary Hotel. I discussed the issue with several of the editors who were among my good media contacts. They understood our policies. But the group voted to recommend that member papers not accept free passes to football games, plays and so forth that had been a tradition for many years. Larger papers generally followed the recommendation. Many still ignore it

Soon after the APME meeting, the *Los Angeles Times* instituted a no freebies policy after a reporter was caught soliciting a free cruise. Editor-in Chief Bill Thomas was an old friend of mine. He and I worked closely for a year when he was the makeup editor for the *Mirror-News* Zone Sections and I was zone editor in the southeast part of the county.

The next time I was in L.A., I went in to see Bill and laid a pair of Disney World passes on his desk, knowing he would probably never get to Florida.

"I brought these all the way from Orlando for you," I said, and got a lecture on the importance of an unbiased press.

Well, gee, I thought Bill had a better sense of humor than that.

Earlier, the *Times'* well-respected travel editor, Jerry Hulse, had visited Walt Disney World, paying his own way. Jerry and I covered the police beat at City Hall in L.A. the first year I worked at the *Mirror-News*. He was on the *Times*. Since our first meeting, Jerry had traveled everywhere, loved Hawaii above every other place and wrote after his stay at our Polynesian Village Hotel, "It's more like Hawaii than Hawaii." You can't buy better publicity than that.

Most newsmen are too smart to be swayed by a few tickets. If they are sent to cover something in a resort attraction like ours, they know either their paper pays or the attraction pays. Either way, it doesn't come out of their pocket, so what's the difference?

There are more effective ways of influencing the press, such as providing exclusive story material that is important to them. And few of them were ever above accepting help in getting a hotel reservation when they were impossible to come by.

That 1973 APME convention, however, was much more famous for another happening at the meeting. That was when President Richard Nixon made his famous "I am not a crook" speech at the Contemporary Hotel.

The White House advance team grudgingly agreed to let us take Mr. Nixon's picture with Mickey Mouse on his arrival, providing it was not released until later. Of course the Nixon family had been with Walt at Disneyland in 1959 for the dedication of the new monorail and at the parks on other occasions.

The speech was broadcast through a pool engineered by CBS. When Nixon walked into the Contemporary Ballroom, the coldness of the crowd was like an ice blanket. It took him at least twenty minutes to generate any sort of reaction except obvious dislike.

Afterwards I told the deputy press secretary that he had missed a bet.

"You should have had him walk in on the arm of Mickey Mouse. It would have brought a laugh and changed the whole atmosphere."

"Oh, no," he replied, "the Presidency is entirely too dignified for that kind of thing."

"For crying out loud," I replied to a startled group of listeners. "He is not an emperor. He is just the President."

The whole press staff blanched white. I still think part of any president's problem is being surrounded by a kind of imperial court in the form of aides and Secret Service who spend as much time protecting his ego and reputation as they do his life.

❧

One other White House celebrity tour was more than memorable. Jimmy Carter's eight-year-old daughter Amy came to visit with a girl friend. They arrived at the Magic Kingdom without parents, but with the usual entourage of Secret Service agents and a Disney VIP hostess.

As they came through the archway into Town Square, the girls spotted Mickey surrounded by at least a hundred eager admirers. With a squeal, the President's daughter dashed away from the Secret Service. She was immediately swallowed up in the crowd, completely invisible among the taller adults for several minutes. The agents obviously panicked, shoving their way to reach their charge.

But Amy was just fine. With a huge grin, she emerged carrying her autograph book with Mickey's signature. She must have done a little shoving of her own to push ahead of others. No one in the crowd was even aware the President's daughter was there. They were too busy with Mickey.

Later Amy and her friend really were in a potentially dangerous situation when we took the two kids for a float-boat trip on Bay Lake to get away from the crowds. The two little girls decided to go up to the front of the boat, which is built like a dining table with pontoons. Separated from her guards by a low railing, the girls dangled their legs in the water.

The boat driver speeded up a little too much and the weight of the girls at the very front and those of the security people a few feet behind caused the front edge of the craft to dip down into the water, which gushed up around the girls' legs.

Secret Servicemen dived forward, causing the boat to tip down even more. The boat driver cut power and the deck righted itself. I could just see the headlines: "President's Daughter in Disney Boat Accident." No harm, no foul.

Her visit and those of many other celebrities helped us build the parks' reputation as a place for celebrities.

❧

The parade of important and ordinary visitors from around the world continued to grow as we expanded. One of the more unusual foreign visits was by the Soyuz cosmonauts when they came to Cape Kennedy to train with the astronauts. Gordon Cooper and many of the other astronauts had come to Walt Disney World frequently to participate in such things as the opening of *Space Mountain* and, very recently, for the opening of *Mission: SPACE* in Epcot.

The Russians, who spoke almost no English, but smiled the whole way, rode *Space Mountain*, the *Jungle Cruise* and other Magic Kingdom favorites, then went to the *Hoop-Dee-Doo Musical Revue* in Fort Wilderness for dinner. They couldn't understand a line of the corny down-home dialogue in the show, but they laughed and sang as loudly as any of the guests who did.

On another occasion, we were posing actress Sophia Loren, who made several visits to the park during the years when her sons were in their early teens, for a picture with Mickey Mouse in front of the Main Street Train Station. Suddenly, a crowd of other guests rushed up and surrounded her. They didn't even recognize Sophia. In fact, they shoved the surprised actress and her two sons aside.

They just wanted to get their own pictures with Mickey.

Chapter 17

Until Michael Eisner arrived in 1984 and instituted major TV advertising programs, Disney relied primarily on free publicity, joint co-op promotions with other companies, and exposure on the Disney television shows. There was no national advertising.

Epcot opened on October 1, 1982 without a single line of newspaper, magazine or television advertising. Yet surveys showed that, by the next morning, ninety percent of Americans knew it had opened.

What our team learned from the opening of Epcot was far more important to the future of our marketing efforts than the event itself, as big as it was. It gave us a unique and slightly accidental opportunity to discover a new thing called satellite transmission.

Months ahead, we were brainstorming for other ways to gain attention. Disney parks marketing was headed by Vice President Jack Lindquist, the most creative marketing mind I ever knew. He must have some of Walt Disney's genes because he could always come up with impossible ideas and find a way to make them work.

But Jack's idea for a full-page ad in newspapers across the country to announce the Epcot opening was turned down cold. We just didn't advertise in those days except for a limited amount of co-op advertising like they did in the motion picture business. The pattern had been set by Walt. So we were doing it that way ever since, with unpaid publicity and a TV show

As compared with future Disney World press events, the plan for Epcot's opening was really small-time. We weren't even aware of the possibility of televising live events without using costly cables.

Suddenly, we discovered *satellite uplinks*, which would change forever the scope of our press events and publicity efforts. This was at a time when local stations were just beginning to install their first satellite receiver dishes, mainly to receive syndicated programs or football games.

Satellite paved the way for some of the largest press events — covered live by more local television stations and radio talk shows — that had ever been attempted by anyone, with the possible exception of political conventions or the Olympics. Up to 226 radio stations, 150 local television news shows, and fifteen thousand invited guests for a single event. If that sounds like bragging, well, I was never shy. And there were several of those between 1982 and 2000.

The logistics for such events were simply amazing. We provided food, lodging and entertainment plus satellite uplinks, edit bays and other tools needed for such broadcasting. Rod Madden, an ex-TV news director on my staff, was responsible for pulling it together with help from technicians from all over the park and leased technical assistance. Hundreds of cast members were involved.

And it all began with one of Jack Lindquist's far-out ideas.

We planned a "soft opening" on October 1, when only limited ceremonies would take place. Our celebrities, key press and VIPs, including top executives from the corporations that sponsored major Epcot attractions, would be invited for the Grand Opening Week — October 15 to 27.

For the October 1 events, Jack wondered if we could hold a unique news conference using coaxial cable links to connect the Epcot ceremonial site with the boardrooms of sponsoring companies so that their presidents could take part. We thought we might also do a closed circuit feed so our people on the West Coast could participate.

As with the Magic Kingdom opening, we wanted to bring the press in small groups between October first and October twenty-fifth so that, by the time of our hour-long Disney TV special on Epcot, the groundwork would be laid. The press would include print media and TV reporters who could shoot film or tape and broadcast it when they returned home.

In our brainstorming session we began to see the possibilities of the new satellite technology.

"Why not do an uplink so stations around the country can pick up our broadcasts for use in local TV news shows?" Jack Lindquist asked. "Would they take such a feed?"

With Walt Disney World Marketing Director Tom Elrod leading the charge, we began surveying local stations to see if they would be interested in sending news crews and doing remote live telecasts from the scene. We would provide an uplink.

We called a few of our news director friends. As it happened, this was also a time when local stations were just beginning to test their new-found capabilities for live remotes in their own areas. This opportunity to have their reporters on the ground for a major event clear across the nation was too good to pass up.

"We'll come!" was the virtually unanimous response.

Television news had totally changed since our opening in 1971, when cameramen arrived with film cameras and sound recorder. They developed the film when they got home. Now ENG (electronic news gathering) was going full blast, so tape was ready for editing immediately. Live news reports were no longer just a network thing.

All three major television networks, sensing huge media interest, committed to sending their own satellite trucks and correspondents for the October first send-off. Soft opening? Not any more.

Some thirty-five stations sent crews, either with their own ENG cameras or using ours. All of them used our single satellite transmitter. We supplied editing facilities and "b-roll," additional footage of attractions that they could not shoot for themselves.

Reporters stood in front of *Spaceship Earth*.

"Here I am, coming to you live from Walt Disney World, where a great new entertainment park opened today."

Immediately, the reporter had scored a coup with the folks back home. Today, when not only Diane Sawyer, but any local news reporter can broadcast live from Baghdad, it would not be a big deal. But back then? Believe me, it was big.

Thirty more stations came during the next two weeks after opening. We kept the uplink in place. Some stations without their own dish borrowed downlinks from PBS stations or university satellite reception dishes.

Many more received our own satellite TV feed that first night and in the days following. That first night, we assigned five-minute segments during the news hour to each station. With three time zones to cover, we could spread them out over a three-hour period.

For the 6 o'clock Eastern Standard casts, however we somehow managed to squeeze fourteen five-minute segments into that single first hour. Clearly some ran a little short.

Back home, TV station switchboards immediately lit up with viewer calls asking for more, praising this new way to get the news. Station managers called their reporters at Walt Disney World.

"Stay longer. Do more reports."

As it had with the Disneyland opening, the extraordinary visual power of Disney attractions brought immediate public response.

Rod Madden recalls that many other stations started calling the next day, asking to send reporters and book satellite time.

"Okay," Rod said, "Give me the coordinates for your receiver."

There was silence. Some didn't know they had to have a receiver to get transmissions from us. That's how new it was.

Rod reminds me that the day Epcot opened was the day the story broke about Tylenol being tampered with, resulting in several deaths. It was a nationwide scare. One station, however, didn't use that as their lead story that night. They had already booked the six to 6:05 p.m. "window" on our satellite uplink and knew it was their only chance during that hour. On that one station at least, death and danger played second fiddle to Mickey Mouse.

Because all of my staff had been touring the country for ten years, making news department friends and contacts, we knew whom to call and they knew us. What's more, they knew they could depend on what we said. For five years, Tom Kennington and his promotion staff had been making similar calls on station managers and program directors in TV and radio.

It was far different from the early days at Disneyland when there was no tape and no satellite. For an opening of a new attraction or new parade back then, we hired a freelance cameraman to come down, shoot a roll of film, go back downtown, edit, make duplicates and deliver to six local stations late that night or early the next day. It was never in time for the six o'clock news on the same day.

Now we could deliver to scores of stations simultaneously and live. Soon it would be hundreds of stations in the U.S. and others in Germany, France, Great Britain, and Japan. In subsequent years, our Disney offices abroad arranged to have scores of foreign TV journalists included in our press events.

When Rod Madden first came to work for me in 1978, one of his first jobs was to cover the Walt Disney World Golf Classic, which was not being carried by network television that year.

"We would send a cameraman to shoot a roll of film on a certain player, bring it back to our truck, develop it and take it down to the Greyhound bus station for delivery to the hometown of the player involved. They usually got it in twenty-four hours. By then the player may have already been eliminated from the Tournament.

"But if we shot on Friday, the station could have its own footage by the time the tourney ended on Sunday. Now there's immediacy for you."

Some of the pro golfers, like Andy Bean, were avid fishermen, so we included shots of them fishing in the streams and ponds around the course at the end of play each day.

As the importance of television news expanded, we began looking for more ways to utilize it as a publicity outlet. Rod came up with a great idea for a newsfilm feature handout on repainting Cinderella Castle.

We showed Cinderella giving her Castle a needed spring cleaning. She began in her urchin's rags, sweeping out the Castle Keep. Some excellent shots taken from a crane showed painters at work hanging from the side of the Castle. Then, with typical Disney magic, Cinderella spun around, pixie dust flew and she emerged wearing her bejeweled ball gown, and the Castle had been transformed with a bright new coat of paint.

We sent it to fifty stations. All used it as a feature story, usually at the end of newscasts. In fact, the results were so good, the following year Rod sent the exact same film to fifty stations in cities where it had not been sent the previous year, with similar results. Again, it was sent by mail.

The new technologies we began using for the first time at the Epcot opening completely revolutionized our publicity efforts, shifting the emphasis from print media to television, especially for openings and other press events. In 1986, with new inspiration and more money from Michael Eisner and Frank Wells, we celebrated our fifteenth anniversary in grand style — fifteen thousand guests, including all three TV morning shows, 115 local TV stations, and 180 radio stations. That doesn't even count the forty or fifty television stations that came from France, Germany, Japan, Great Britain, Italy and other countries that send thousands of overseas visitors to Walt Disney World each year.

For the occasion, we leased twelve satellite trucks, at $3,500 a pop, fully equipped with personnel, all the electronic gear and up links. Tom Cormier, who had been recruited by Rod from a relatively uninteresting job in our telephone company, provided technical coordination and helped in arranging for the TV trucks. We used virtually every one available in the eastern United States! It was an amazing job of coordination. Tom was one of the few who had the technical know-how to do it back then.

Each fall, when anniversaries and openings frequently took place, we always had to avoid having transmissions on Saturday because those trucks were tied up with network football coverage.

Radio generally sent their morning show, drive time or talk

show hosts. At least sixty radio stations broadcast simultaneously. Another who played a major role in bringing in and handling radio stations was Tom Darren. He gave me the figures. For the twenty-fifth anniversary party in 1996, we hosted 226 radio stations. Forty stations were located in each park — Magic Kingdom, Epcot and Disney-MGM Studios.

The next day, another hundred took their place. We supplied tented booths at central locations in each park. They supplied the talent.

We also supplied planners, operations, entertainment and marketing personnel as interview subjects. The job of handling all of the transportation and hospitality chores, planning food and entertainment, coordinating the scheduling of interviews, providing escorts to show station personnel where to go, even in the wee hours of the morning, plus providing edit bays, press kits, press room facilities and all the other support for such an event required thousands of Disney cast members. Many were working totally outside their field of expertise.

Mary Haupt, then in Human Relations, conducted classes for escorts and interviewees, five hundred to six hundred in a single session at one of our ballrooms. Later she created a whole department, which operates full-time to handle many events. Guest Relations hosts, accustomed to conducting tours of the property, were in the forefront. But finance, marketing, legal, human relations, and all the other backstage divisions with cast members not needed for daily operations sent people to help.

Rod Madden helped set up all of the TV support facilities. My secretary, Sandra Broulliard, headed up press room arrangements. She was later in charge of scheduling interviews, an impossible job before the days of computers. Tom Elrod's marketing team, with Jack Lindquist looking in to supply upper-level guidance and inspiration from his California office, led the way, but every member in the Walt Disney World cast — which grew from ten thousand to more than fifty thousand over the twenty years following the Epcot opening — was a vital cog.

Events, some smaller than others but always major, were held for opening other new attractions in Epcot — *Living Seas, Imagination!, Wonders of Life, Test Track, Mission: SPACE*, Morocco, Norway, and *Soarin'* — the Grand Floridian Resort and ten other Disney hotels, then Disney-MGM Studios, two water parks, Downtown Disney, Mickey Mouse and Donald Duck's Birthdays, Disney's Animal Kingdom and many more, not to mention the Tokyo, Paris and Hong Kong Disney resorts.

The 1955 opening of Disneyland had set the pattern for all the later openings — a spectacular ceremony with celebrities and parades and a television special. Many times the entertainment was primarily for the benefit of the attending press. Many included famous dignitaries as participants. In 1959 it was Vice President Richard Nixon and family plus a parade led by Meredith Willson, but Walt himself was the biggest star attraction throughout his lifetime. In 1966, Walt presided at ceremonies for the openings of *It's a Small World* and New Orleans Square.

Since no one could replace Walt as *the* star, our later grand openings required multiple stars to create the same impact. Many of them agreed to participate in the Walt Disney World opening, I'm sure, because of their respect for Walt — Julie Andrews, Bob Hope, Glen Campbell, Buddy Hackett, Jonathan Winters and Meredith Willson, again leading the parade of seventy-six trombones as he had at Disneyland in 1959. The result was a spectacular television special and an event that sent our press guests away saying, "No one does it like Disney."

In 1975, for the opening of *Space Mountain* and *Pirates of the Caribbean* at Walt Disney World, our publicity was focused on six of the Apollo astronauts, who brought their Moon Rover as part of the show. Luci Arnaz and Tommy Tune starred in the accompanying TV show. Later that year, *America On Parade*, with fifty floats and one hundred fifty Disney characters, began its year-long run celebrating America's Bicentennial with a major press event, a gala night in downtown Orlando and the appearance of Supreme Court Chief Justice Warren Burger. We had about one thousand media representatives hosted for the event.

Singer John Davidson starred in the opening of *Big Thunder Mountain Railroad* in 1980, which included another major gathering of press from around the nation.

Epcot's Grand Opening for three thousand invited guests plus one thousand press featured Danny Kaye, the West Point Glee Club, performing groups from twenty-three nations, the Glenn Miller, Bob Crosby, Lionel Hampton, Count Basie and Pete Fountain bands, and the dedication of the new park by Disney Chairman E. Cardon Walker and Mrs. Walt Disney. The events started getting bigger with the arrival of Michael D. Eisner as Disney chairman, beginning with the Grand Floridian Beach Resort gala opening with Burt Reynolds, Loni Anderson, Astronaut Gordon Cooper and The Beach Boys.

Because Disneyland is a family entertainment place, Walt always encouraged us to include families — at least wives — in all of our press events and trips. And we brought our own wives along to help host press. It started with those family picnics for a few hundred invitees and grew at Walt Disney World into those mammoth press events with up to fifteen thousand guests for whom we had to arrange lodging, transportation, entertainment, elaborate meals — usually outside in places like World Showcase, which was one of the few sites big enough — plus all kinds of press materials and facilities for editing and transmitting newspaper, radio and television stories.

Because of our arrangements with Eastern and then Delta Airlines, for many years we were able to provide free or reduced rate transportation as well as accommodations on the property. I doubt if any company ever came close to the scope of those events in the 1980s, '90s and into the new millennium.

The results were always astounding to me, so much bigger than we could have imagined when we first started inviting those six opening-month press groups in October 1971. Then, arrangements for the press were handled almost entirely by our little publicity group. And we were the ones who took them on tour and answered their questions. Now we recruited executives and spokespeople from throughout the resort to assist.

For another grand opening at Epcot, the press stayed dry but the principle ribbon-cutter got soaked.

The first new attraction completed soon after Michael Eisner and Frank Wells joined the company was *The Living Seas*, completed in 1986. It included one of the world's largest aquarium tanks, so vast you could look through viewing windows on one side and never see the opposite wall of the tank. We decided to stage an underwater ribbon-cutting with Mickey Mouse.

Press guests were seated in the Coral Reef Café, which had foot-thick windows with a clear view of all the fish, including sharks, manta rays and thousands of brightly colored tropical fish. Mickey was dressed in full scuba diving gear. In a graphic display of his sportsmanship and willingness to flaunt the usual rules of executive decorum, Wells volunteered to don his own scuba gear and help Mickey cut the ribbon.

Underwater microphones enabled opening day guests and covering press to hear Mickey and Frank make the dedication while talking with Michael Eisner on the dry side of the glass.

As a matter of fact, scuba diving was only one aspect of Wells' adventurous nature. He had been an avid mountain climber ever since his days as a Rhodes Scholar in England. Soon after completing the scholarship, he and a friend flew a small airplane to the top of Mt. Kilimanjaro when he conceived the idea of scaling the highest peak on each of the seven continents.

His expedition to Mt. Everest just before taking the Disney job was the final leg of his quest. To make the expedition, Wells had taken several months leave of absence from his prior position as president of Warner Bros. Studios. Everest eluded him, but he was offered the Disney position soon after his return from Nepal.

Chapter 18

$\mathcal{A}$s a part of the marketing team, I helped plan press coverage for many other Grand Openings. Perhaps the most memorable for me was the opening of Disneyland Paris, originally called Euro Disney. I had spent three weeks in Paris in 1989 helping set up a press conference for unveiling detailed plans for the new resort, with five hotels designed by world-class architects plus a Magic Kingdom even more lavish than those that preceded it.

I remember trying with little success to herd eager photographers jockeying to get pictures of a whole array of scale models of the buildings. That's tough when you don't speak more than three words of French.

Two years later, after trying to learn enough French to get along (by listening to tapes), I went to France for a year to set up the publicity department. It was the most memorable year of my life. Gretta took early retirement from her job as a junior high school principal's secretary. We moved in the fall of 1991 to a rented house near the ancient village of Bussy St. George, next to a new golf course about three miles from Disneyland Paris at Marne-le-Vallee. Beautiful old French chateaux were all around.

I chose that rural location and spacious house over living in a tiny Parisian apartment in the heart of the city, a long commute from the construction site every day. We were only twenty miles east of downtown Paris so we could easily drive into the city for dining or shopping. Paris had long been my favorite city of the many I visited, so this was already the opportunity of a lifetime.

The new resort and park were scheduled to open in April of 1992. We began making press contacts all over Europe and Great Britain and sending out stories about the much-anticipated project. The publicity build-up was moving well.

But it wasn't always easy. Paris in springtime may be ideal, but Paris in the winter is wet, cold and constantly gray. I spent days walking the construction site wearing heavy rubber boots and sloshing through mud. A vintage paddlewheel steamboat was completed in November, but ice on the Rivers of America prevented taking pictures of it in motion for more than a month. We finally photographed it sailing around *Big Thunder Mountain Railroad*, which also was rapidly taking final form.

One way to let press know what was coming was to bring them for site tours in very small groups. Another was a four-color tabloid "newspaper" that I edited. I took quite a few pictures for it myself as I went around gathering story material. Our Disney Imagineers were constantly fighting deadlines, so finding time for them to explain the details of each project to me was never easy.

For pre-opening, the park had two French staff photographers plus Alain Boniec, whom I borrowed for three months from the Walt Disney World photography department. Alain was a great help because, having been born in France, he spoke the language and could be my official translator, a very necessary role.

Most French people who became part of the Disneyland Paris cast spoke English so it was not totally necessary for me to learn the language well. Although, as with many two-language interchanges, difficulty in translation can lead to a lot of misunderstandings. Many times I would explain something, and the other person would nod his understanding. Later I would realize he had gotten it all wrong.

The Disney representatives in many European cities were a vital help in spreading the word on the new resort. I also went on many mission trips, as I had in the U.S., to meet travel writers and editors in their home offices, not a common practice in Europe. They usually wanted to meet outside the office.

The anticipation among the press surrounding the new park was tremendous and mostly favorable except for a relatively small segment of French cultural writers. Unfortunately they are also the ones who are close to American correspondents in Paris, so whatever they wrote was picked up in the United States — things like the French cultural minister calling Disneyland Paris a "cultural Chernobyl." That one caught U.S. newspaper readers' attention all right. Most Frenchmen, I felt, paid very little attention to that parochial attitude. They came by the millions after we opened, regardless of any supposed culture clash.

But that elite segment of writers, and I met several of them, seem to think they are descendants of the French nobility who lost their heads to the guillotine and must personally preserve the cultural integrity of the nation. Nevertheless, the vast majority of publicity we got on television radio and in newspapers throughout Europe prior to opening was not only favorable but darned near ecstatic.

The opening was a grand event attended by thousands of newspeople and celebrities.

Not that I claim a connection, but the negative press and the financial troubles, which have dogged Disneyland Paris since it opened, didn't start until after I left. Maybe the build-up was just too much. I have always operated on the principle of promising a little and delivering a lot when it comes to the media.

But sometimes, the build-up just gains momentum no matter what you do.

Although attendance at the Disneyland Paris Magic Kingdom was generally well ahead of pre-opening *pro-formas*, spending on food and merchandise and the hotel occupancy rate both fell far below projections. The *pro forma* was also based on being able to develop large areas of the "New City" site as laid out by the French government with large-scale commercial development of office buildings, apartments and shopping.

Unfortunately, by the time the new Disney resort opened, demand for commercial property had hit rock bottom. It was impossible to move forward, so the entire financial load of building the project fell on proceeds from the Magic Kingdom. That meant huge financial difficulties that still have not been completely overcome, although a large up-scale shopping center, a factory outlet mall and several residential developments have been added with considerable success in recent years.

One obvious change was made early on in order to attract more people for meals in the park. As we had at Disneyland under Walt's guidance, no alcoholic beverages were served in the Magic Kingdom park, although drinks were served in the hotels. But Europeans just didn't want their meals without beer or wine. The no-alcohol policy was changed after a few months.

Thank goodness all of that happened after I left. I have returned several times since for a visit and still believe Disneyland Paris is one of the world's great entertainment achievements, second only to Walt Disney World. The French Magic Kingdom still ranks as Europe's most popular attraction, with twice as many visitors as Versailles or the Eiffel Tower.

Disneyland Paris was the first place I felt needed a Media Guide Book for the opening, one printed in several languages. Such "Press Books" were traditionally developed for major motion picture publicity efforts in Hollywood. But we had never felt the need for anything but a smaller press kit with a collection of stories, pictures and fact sheets in the U.S.

This time, I felt a Press Book would be helpful because everything was so new and different for our European media audience. Although nearly everyone had heard about our other Disney parks, only a small percentage of the press in Europe had ever seen Disneyland or Walt Disney World.

The Press Book, unlike promotional brochures, was a working tool with a collection of key stories and all the facts we could gather about the new project, its park, hotels, recreation areas and infrastructure. An index made it easy for the press to find necessary information to use in writing stories.

Writing Press Books turned out to be the one big thing I did for Disney after "retirement."

In 1996, while still working full-time as a "consultant," I collected as much history about Walt Disney World as I could assemble and created a similar Media Guide for the resort's twenty-fifth anniversary. It brought back a lot of great memories for me. It gives an outline of all the parks, hotels, attractions and recreational facilities, opening dates, visiting celebrities and recollections of "old timers."

In 1998, after going on a part-time consultancy basis, I wrote the Media Guide for the opening of Disney's Animal Kingdom, helped with its opening and, three years later, wrote another similar guide for the opening of Disney's California Adventure and Grand Californian Hotel in Anaheim.

My most recent Media Guide writing, and perhaps the last, was for the Grand Opening of Hong Kong Disneyland in 2005. I was able to complete the book during a two-week visit to China in April. Fortunately, I timed it so I could be on hand for the May opening of Disneyland's Fiftieth Anniversary celebration.

Rapid changes in technology are opening vast new doors for Disney publicity efforts. Toward the end of 2003, I was merely a guest at the beginning of Mickey Mouse's Seventy-Fifth Anniversary year when Michael Eisner unveiled seventy-five statues created by artists and celebrities in tribute to Mickey.

That day, I'm told, Walt Disney World's news feed from the event via satellite was broadcast more than twelve hundred times on TV stations and cable networks in the U.S. within twenty-four hours. And that's only the ones that could be immediately verified. Who knows how many more were used overseas?

But all that publicity success can be traced back to the beginning — to Walt Disney, Eddie Meck and that wild "press preview" in 1955.

Perhaps I should explain my use of the term *publicity*. In Europe, publicity means advertising. For us, it means press relations and promoting the unpaid use of information about Disney parks in newspapers, magazines, radio and television. After making several changes in name – including media relations -- my old department is now called *Public Relations*. I guess *press* is old-fashioned and doesn't really include radio and TV. Somehow *media relations* sound slightly illicit to me, but as usual I'm just old-fashioned enough to like the term *press agent* or even *press relations*.

I love to play with words, which led to my main claim to fame when it comes to naming new things for the Disney parks. Name choosing was always our most difficult task. It was always nearly impossible for a roomful of planners to agree on any one name for anything. But you have to have a name before you can write a press release about anything, so the choice has to come early.

Thank God, Walt never had any trouble making those kinds of choices. Over the years I made many suggestions for naming new attractions or events. Early on I had some success taking part in inventing *Tencennial* as the name for Disneyland's tenth anniversary. Later I think I had a hand in helping Walt Disney Imagineering (WDI) choose the name for the Seven Seas Lagoon at Walt Disney World.

WDI ordinarily handles the name selection as a part of creating new attractions. Like Walt, Michael Eisner was very good at making the final choice among names developed by the Imagineers. So I was pleased when he chose one of my suggestions.

In 1994, Michael was looking for a unique name for his pet project, a huge exposition of new technologies and hi-tech systems to replace *CommuniCore* at the center of Epcot's Future World. Many top companies had signed on to present mind-boggling demonstrations of their newest products and inventions.

New inventions and innovations seemed the key ingredients. So I decided to combine the two words and suggested *Innoventions*. Michael liked it immediately and the name stuck.

There were a few such battles I lost, however, like my effort to get rid of the term "theme park." I always felt the term was not a whole lot better than "amusement park." Both are too ordinary to describe a Disneyland type park. I prefer to call them *Disney Parks*, which rightly places them in a class by themselves. Although Michael and others have agreed, we were never able to get copywriters and others in the company to get rid of *theme parks*.

Another term never intended as a permanent name was *Contemporary Hotel*. When Roy Disney first announced what hotels we would build in Phase I, they were generic designations like Polynesian style (not too bad for a name), an Asian hotel (okay), Venetian Hotel (so-so), Persian hotel (Persia is no more) and a "contemporary" hotel.

By the time the first two were completed, we were so used to calling them the Polynesian and the Contemporary Hotel that Imagineers couldn't seem to come up with another name that had any degree of acceptance among top Disney people.

While Walt Disney World was still under construction, a Miami columnist wrote he heard one of our hotels was going to be called the "Temporary Hotel." With the usual competitive Miami attitude, he thought making the hotel temporary would be a good thing.

In recent years, outside experts have been hired, focus groups polled and the name picking process has become really "scientific" but no easier. Still, in the final analysis, one guy has to make the big choices. For now, I guess it's up to the new CEO, Bob Iger.

On the job at Disneyland Paris. Behind every great parade is a publicity guy making sure everything steps off according to plan, monitoring closely but ducking down so as not to spoil guest views.

Chapter 19

When Frank Wells and Michael Eisner came to Disney in 1984, it was almost like Walt was back. They began by shaking hands with virtually the entire cast in a walk-through down Main Street. That was like Walt.

After years in which the company was threatened with outside takeover, the movies were doing badly, and we were struggling to keep up with the public's demands for hotels and new attractions, it was wonderful to find new leaders with imagination and enthusiasm making the right choices.

Go-aheads for the Grand Floridian and the Swan-Dolphin projects were among the first decisions made by Eisner after taking over and realizing the extent of the hotel room shortage. In a few short years, we increased the tally from five thousand to well over thirty thousand rooms on property.

Plans for the Disney-MGM Studios park soon materialized, itself an exciting concept. Many of us, having experienced the thrill of visiting Hollywood studios that generally were closed to the public, recognized its potential when Michael first announced it. In fact, Walt had anticipated that idea in his original plan for Disneyland, adapting techniques from the design of movie sets. He had hoped to make films there. That never happened because shooting a movie with ten thousand guests looking on didn't seem practical until Disney Imagineering figured ways to control public viewing of production at Disney-MGM Studios.

In other parts of the company, *Wonderful World of Disney* was back on the air with Michael as host. A new era of animation started with big musical films like *The Little Mermaid, Aladdin, The Lion King, Beauty and the Beast* and all the others. That gave us a fresh new set of characters for shows, parades and personal appearances, plus great music, which has always been a vital Disney element.

Less than five years into the Eisner-Wells era, as we neared the opening of the Studios park and two major hotels, Michael was ready to announce even bigger future plans for the 1990s. Tom Elrod labeled it the *Disney Decade*.

That's when I discovered *advanced planning by press release*. We set up a transcontinental press trip for the announcements. We flew our eastern media to California for the beginning of Disneyland's thirty-fifth birthday celebration. Then, in chartered DC-9s, we took both East and West Coast press back to Florida for the opening of the Swan Hotel, designed by famous architect Michael Graves. Each coast scheduled major press conferences announcing the ten-year *Disney Decade* plan, first for Disneyland and later for Walt Disney World.

In early January 1989, I flew to California to sit down with Michael and write the press releases covering those *Disney Decade* plans for Walt Disney World. He outlined several new hotels, major new attractions in the parks, a "fourth gate" (which became Disney's Animal Kingdom), a new water park, more golf courses and much more. A second park for Anaheim was also in the plan. Disney's California Adventure opened in 2001, the only major project to miss the Decade deadline.

Disney-MGM Studios was already nearly completed. We worked over each paragraph with great care. Many times Michael would say, "Now the Imagineers don't know about this project, but we will do it." And for the most part every one of those projects came to fruition and more.

One project he decided to leave out of the announcement at the last minute was labeled *Hollywood Terror Hotel*. We had artist renderings and a sketchy outline of a new thriller at the Studios park — "a mysterious hotel that had been struck by lightning and deserted." With major improvements, it ultimately became the Disney-MGM Studios' most popular attraction, *The Twilight Zone Tower of Terror.*

Michael decided the idea was too good — someone might steal it. So we destroyed the stories and stuck the artists' rendering photos back on file — all but one. Somehow, one print got left in the pressroom by mistake. An *Orlando Sentinel* reporter found it.

All he had to go on was the caption that labeled it the *Hollywood Hotel.* I'm sure he was afraid to ask about it because he knew he wasn't supposed to have the picture. The next day, the *Sentinel* story about the *Disney Decade* was accompanied by illustrations, including an artist's rendering of what the *Sentinel* said would be a new hotel near the Studios park — Hollywood Hotel.

Frankly, I'm sorry we didn't build a haunted hotel. With proper squeaking doors and disappearing pictures, I think ghost lovers would have kept the hotel full forever.

One of Michael Eisner's first moves in 1984 focused on revolutionizing marketing. He named a new marketing planning group called the MATADORS — an acronym for **M**arketing and **A**dmissions **T**eam **A**ssigned to **D**isney **O**bjectives of **R**apidly **S**ucceeding. (Thank God, no one ever asked us to spell it out.)

The MATADOR meetings, with Frank and Michael at the helm, were pure excitement. Twenty or so managers and creative heads sat around a crowded conference table spewing wild promotional ideas in every direction.

Michael wanted to revolutionize our old marketing concepts by adding major national and regional advertising programs. By pure coincidence, Marketing VP Tom Elrod was ready with the results of a unique target market program tested in the weeks before Eisner arrived. The "targets" were Houston, Kansas City and Boston, where publicity, promotion *and* advertising were concentrated for a three-week test period. The plan involved personal appearances in each market by Disney spokespeople and characters, radio and TV contests offering trips to Walt Disney World, and spot TV commercials.

The tests had been highly successful, prompting Eisner to commit $4 million for a broader test in twenty major markets. Focus groups were formed to help develop effective commercials. Successful results prompted the development of major national and local spot advertising and promotional programs involving millions of dollars. Highlights included tours by hot air balloons in the shape of Mickey Mouse and Donald Duck, and events such as one in Boston where the whole city seemed to turn out for a parade of Disney characters, presented with the help of the city's largest department store and a local TV station.

The results, in terms of attendance and hotel occupancy, were fabulous.

Not everything went smoothly for the MATADORS in those first weeks.

One huge publicity crisis caused near panic. The word came during our second MATADOR meeting with Frank and Michael. The famous Radio City Rockettes were picketing Mickey Mouse, marching around New York's famed Radio City Music Hall carrying signs declaring, "Mickey Mouse is a Rat."

It seems Disney had arranged with Radio City to produce a Christmas spectacular featuring Snow White and the Seven Dwarfs for the month of December. It would replace the Rockettes' traditional Christmas show. The dancers were furious. They kept on marching for days.

There was consternation among the MATADORS. What could we do? The show was committed. Jack Lindquist suggested a full-page ad in the *New York Times* defending our Mouse. At one point we were nearly committed to sending Mickey with his own marching band to confront the protesters in the middle of the Avenue of the Americas.

Cooler heads prevailed. We started negotiations, which resulted in the Rockettes coming to Walt Disney World the following year to stage a summer-long Red, White and Blue dance extravaganza. It provided plenty of favorable publicity, a big boost for park attendance and a salve for the New York dancers' wounded pride, although not without sacrifice on their part. They danced on an open stage at World Showcase through three months of mid-summer Florida heat, enduring sudden showers, which turned the stage floor into an ice-slick surface.

The most startling accomplishment of the MATADORS was when one brainstorm led the marketing team to become architects and builders of what was to be one of the most popular new areas in the Magic Kingdom's most successful attractions.

Originally called Mickey's Birthdayland (now Mickey's Toontown Fair), it began as a temporary new land to celebrate Mickey's Sixtieth Birthday in 1988.

More than a year before, the Entertainment Division began planning Mickey's Sixtieth Birthday Parade as a procession of characters down Main Street, U.S.A., but we wanted a stronger hook for our publicity efforts. We thought about erecting a tent in the employee parking area behind Main Street where guests could come for a party and meet Mickey and other characters. Artists accustomed to drawing for advertisements and brochures were called in to help visualize it in renderings — people like Don "Ducky" Williams, whose specialty was drawing Disney characters.

They came up with an idea for a red and white striped tent with a stage for a musical show, then added a concept for Mickey's house, a 1920s-style bungalow with his balloon-tired car sitting outside. There could be, we thought, an air-filled balloon of Mickey thirty feet high as an icon and some simple little playgrounds and fountains for younger kids. We felt there was a shortage of things for the under-school-age children.

Marketing VP Tom Elrod took the idea to Michael Eisner. He liked it and turned it over to Walt Disney Imagineering for study and refinement. Totally tied up with designing and building the Disney-MGM Studios park at the time, the Imagineers asked for a delay and advised moving the site to the new park, with an opening date well after 1989.

We were disappointed. We still needed a marketing hook for Mickey's Birthday in 1988. So the MATADORS kept thinking about it. More artists' drawings were made. A possible site was picked in an unused corner of Fantasyland. Maintenance planners were pulled into the brainstorming sessions. We decided to create a new depot and have a *Walt Disney World Railroad* stop at Mickey's land. The steam engine was redecorated as Mickey's Birthday Express. A red-striped tent could be purchased as a unit for much less time and money than building a permanent structure. Leaping fountains would create a small water play area nearby.

Tom Elrod flew to California to present Michael with "The New Plan." By then it was February. Mickey's Birthday was in November. The maintenance guys said it could be finished by then, by the skin of our knuckles. We had a budget — $12 million — about one-tenth of what major new attractions were costing by that time.

It didn't take long to get a decision, but it came with a shocking requirement.

"You can do it," Michael said at the end of a half-day session, "but it must be finished by May so it will have a positive effect on summer season attendance."

That kind of inspired decision was pure "Walt Disney."

Could it be done? Tom called from California and got my friend Tom Garrison, who had been named to ride herd on the project. Garrison started as a studio publicist at the same time that I joined Ed Meck's staff. Later, he was in the operations departments at Disneyland and Disney World before coming back to marketing as a liaison with operations and other departments and director of marketing personnel.

Garrison called his contacts in maintenance construction.

"Can do. We think."

The word was "go" — in a hurry.

Land clearance began the next day. I don't know how many un-sung heroes there were, but I do know it was an extraordinary effort by many tremendously creative and hardworking people doing some-thing they had never tried before. The plastic tent was purchased and erected. Engineers came up with an innovative plan to air-condition the tent using huge concrete storm-drain pipes to carry cold air un-derground to the tent. Artists began adding details to their draw-ings. There were not many blueprints. There simply wasn't time.

Draftsmen added plans for electricity and plumbing to the de-signs. Workmen began building a funky little California bungalow with a sagging roof as *Mickey's Country House*. The hurried imagina-tion of the substitute architects from marketing produced a giant bed with Mickey's tux and his red flannel underwear hanging on the bedposts. There was a small kitchen splattered with paint by Goofy's redecorating attempts, a living room with an old-fashioned TV set showing Mickey Mouse cartoons — all kinds of weird and appealing furnishings.

The whole marketing team chipped in with wild ideas. One was a "theater" for Mickey's dressing room where guests could be as-sured of meeting and getting their pictures taken with Mickey. People always wanted pictures with Mickey. There must have been magic mirrors involved because no one ever saw more than one Mickey, but we were able to triple the number of greetings with the famous mouse.

Crews worked 'round the clock. Garrison got calls at home in the middle of the night.

"Are you sure this is where it goes?"

Tom answered yes and listened for the sound of the hammer driving the nail. Because of overtime it went over budget — about $14 million, I heard — but it was completed in time for dedication by Mrs. Nancy Reagan and other dignitaries in May.

The place was a giant success at a fraction of the usual cost of a new attraction or new land resulting from years of planning. More than seventy percent of all visitors spent time in Mickey's Birthdayland in the first year.

It was originally planned as a temporary attraction, but Michael soon decided to change the name to Mickey's Starland and make it permanent. It was a prime example of the Eisner-Wells team's ability to seize on a good idea and move fast, allowing talented people to carry it out.

Disney Imagineers subsequently took the idea, expanded it, spent a hundred million dollars or so, and created Mickey's Toontown at Disneyland, then came back to Florida in 1996 with many improvements, including *Minnie's Country House, Donald's Boat* and *The Barnstormer at Goofy's Wiseacre Farm*. It was then renamed Mickey's Toontown Fair at Disney World.

Mickey's Birthdayland probably could not be built today with all the financial analyzers sitting on top of it — certainly not in the same way. That kind of shoot-from-the-hip management, so typical of Michael and Frank at the time, was what made everything fun, exciting and — big surprise — "successful."

Wells and Eisner were an unbeatable team. When Frank was killed in a helicopter crash during a ski trip in 1994, it was nearly as traumatic for me as when Walt died. I am sure it was the same for Michael and many others.

Chapter 20

When I began working for Disney in 1963, we didn't have cell phones, Xerox copiers, fax machines, video tape recorders or computers. We printed our press releases using mimeograph stencils taken to the "mail room" and run off on rotary press mimeograph machines. We got our mailing list from visiting press, personal contacts and the *Editor and Publisher* yearbook. Addresses were stored on metal plates run by hand using a machine that fed the addressograph plates and envelopes through with an ink ribbon to transfer the addresses.

Even when we went to Florida, our first computerized mailing list used orange IBM punch cards which had to be punched and then sent to California for sorting on the Studio's room-sized RCA computers so a set of labels could be printed. It took a week. Every time a name changed on our list, a new card was punched.

Today, we can do it all on a desktop computer in an hour. Until about 1980, most of the staff depended on electric typewriters, which I could never use. I composed on the typewriter. Every time I rested my fingers to think, a splatter of letters came out of the electric monster. That required minutes to cover with "white out." If you needed a few copies, you put layers of carbon paper in the typewriter. To avoid my electric nemesis, I used an old Royal manual typewriter for twenty more years until I finally learned to use a computer. What a speed-up in creative writing!

For communications within Disneyland, there was two-way radio, but we seldom had access to it because it was so over-crowded with operations traffic. We got very good at walking rapidly through the park, glancing in every direction to find the whereabouts of a co-worker or a celebrity on tour.

When Rod Madden came to work for me in 1976, he recalls, we still didn't have fax machines. We could send material over the phone lines on a Quip machine but it took six minutes to send one page — *if* it was set on high speed. Now we can send a whole story via the Internet in seconds.

New technology seemed to spur fresh new marketing ideas.

For Disneyland's Thirtieth Birthday, Jack Lindquist came up with a plan for one of Disneyland's most successful promotions — giving away a progressively more valuable gift to every thirtieth, three-hundredth and three-thousandth visitor. Every thirty-thousandth visitor received a General Motors car. They used computerized turnstiles to identify winning guests. General Motors helped promote it with their dealers and GM cars were displayed at the park entrance for the year.

It was so successful that in 1986, for Walt Disney World's Fifteenth Anniversary, a General Motors car was given away *every day* during the year. That got their attention.

Perhaps the most innovative promotional idea to arise during those days when the door for new ideas was wide open came not from Michael but from his wife Jane. Forevermore it would be called, "What's Next?"

Jane and Michael were dining with a pair of aerial pioneers who had just become instant celebrities by setting a record for navigating the world without stopping or refueling. Pilots Dick Rutan and Jeana Yeager had landed their Voyager aircraft at Edwards Air Force Base in December 1996. The Eisner meeting came less than a month later.

In casual conversation, Jane asked, "Now that you have been around the world, what are you going to do next?"

Jokingly the pilots replied, "We're going to Disneyland." And there it was!

"What a great idea for a Disney commercial," was Jane's automatic reaction.

The concept was inspired but the execution, which was totally incredible, surprised everyone.

The next morning Michael was on the phone to Tom Elrod in Florida. Superbowl XXI was just two weeks away.

"Turn it on," Michael ordered.

Tom literally grabbed the ball and ran with it to the National Football League.

The NFL agreed immediately to support the idea of having the hero of the game participate. Appearance fees were arranged with likely candidates from the New York Giants and the Denver Broncos. NFL Films agreed to supply game footage within an hour of the end of the game in the Rose Bowl.

Some might have been content to tape a commercial to run a week or month later — not Michael. He wanted it on the air the next day.

Perhaps no one deserves more credit for pulling it off than Maureen O'Donnell, a slender, almost timid-looking, middle-aged Creative Services production scheduler keeping track of the daily flow of newspaper, radio and television ads, promotional brochures and the like.

With an ENG camera crew in tow, she stood poised on the sidelines, barely waiting until the final whistle to dash onto the field, elbowing her way through fans and interview-hungry TV newsmen to grab New York Giants quarterback Phil Simms by the jersey.

Edited in later, the booming voice of an announcer shouts over the screaming uproar of a just-finished championship game:

"Phil Simms, now that you have won the Super Bowl, what are you going to do next?" Phil had just two lines to record.

"I'm going to Disney World!" and "I'm going to Disneyland!"

One was for the East Coast, one for the West. Losing quarterback John Elway had to wait another eleven years for his chance to be asked, "What's Next?"

Next came the real miracle! The completed TV spot was aired less than twelve hours later on *Good Morning America* over the ABC-TV network, on New York, Los Angeles and Denver television stations and in many other NFL cities across the country.

As arranged, Quarterback Simms and his family were touring Disneyland that day with broad grins and wordless endorsement. Madison Avenue was bowled over. The surprise of the commercial made almost as much news on television and in many newspapers as the recap of the game itself.

In the twenty years since, "What's Next?" has almost become an art form. All across the country Little Leaguers and other sports winners can be heard to shout in their moments of triumph — "I'm going to Disney World!"

Within a few weeks after Simms had delivered his victory line, Maureen had flown to Australia for America's Cup Skipper Dennis Connors to join the celebration. The tape was edited on the plane coming back and transmitted from Hawaii, still just the next morning after the race. The Lakers' Magic Johnson and Minnesota Twins World Series hero Frank Viola took their turns the same year.

Thirty-one other celebrities have carried on the "What's Next?" tradition, including two twentieth anniversary heroes, Hines Ward and Jerome Bettis of the Pittsburgh Steelers.

Each year produced additional news stories about what has become a classic event of its own. The one year, 2005, when Disney decided to skip the spot, there was a spate of comment about its absence. Some people just don't like change.

American styles and cultural climate for publicity have changed in radical ways since the Disneyland debut in 1955. In the old days, we would invite press to review shows and concerts at Disneyland, saving a place up front for our press VIPs, who frequently came in after a large crowd had arrived. It was accepted as a matter of course.

But, beginning around 1970, as I was moving to Florida, that tolerant spirit changed. Our late arrivers were loudly booed, causing us to place our reserved seats farther back or to one side or to not have reserved seats at all.

Disneyland originally had many "backdoor" entrances used for celebrities out of a fear that having celebs waiting in line would lead to problems with autograph seekers. Dignitaries and celebrities were also frequently on tight time schedules. But, as public resentment to such special privilege rose, the use of backdoors was reduced to the most unusual cases, with new methods being used to obscure public views of celebrity guests.

Detroit travel writer Rick Sylvain was always getting into unusual places. Ten years after I snapped this picture of him in Egypt, he came to work for me at WDW. By then, we had adopted the same no-smoking policy as the ancient pyramids.

Chapter 21

$\mathcal{I}$ was definitely with Disney at the right time for me. I got to know Walt and meet show business stars, royalty, celebrated news people and guests from all walks of life. They were there for fun, which made our hosting job easy. My job gave me a chance to become an associate member of the Society of American Travel Writers, which is made up of tremendously creative people who manage to hold their annual conventions in far off exotic travel destinations. I went with them at least thirty times to places I had only dreamed of visiting, like Australia, Egypt, Hungary, Spain, Brazil, Thailand, Switzerland, Poland, Croatia and many more.

Among many memorable conventions was one in Israel in 1983 with a pre-convention trip to Egypt, where I came within a buggy-wheel turn of sudden death along with Rick Sylvain, then travel editor of the *Detroit Free Press*. We ran into each other at the Hilton Hotel on the east bank of the Nile River after a day of wandering around the bazaars and museums of Cairo. We needed to go to our own hotel in Giza on the other side of the river and decided to take a horse-drawn carriage. We thought it would be something of an adventure but we got more than we bargained for.

It was dusk as we headed across a sixteen-lane bridge crossing the Nile with an island park in the middle of the stream. Bumper to bumper traffic was moving at a steady pace in all lanes when our horse suddenly spooked and took off at a gallop, dodging in and out among the cars, totally out of control. We were too scared to yell.

The driver — if he spoke English I never knew — shouted at

the horse, pulled on the reins, maneuvered him into a narrow lane on the right hand side and managed to turn down an empty off ramp onto the island. It took a long block before he could calm the horse to a walk.

The carriage took a circular route and wound up back in front of the Hilton Hotel. There may be nothing more stupid than seasoned travelers too proud to avoid danger. Like fools, we stayed on board while the carriage took us without further incident back to our hotel. I never quite realized how close we came until I got back home and started telling the story.

As if that wasn't enough, Rick and I joined forces again, renting a car for a post-convention trip from Jerusalem to the Red Sea and back to Tel Aviv to rejoin the travel writers for the return flight. We saw Jericho, the Dead Sea, Elat, Ben Gurion's rural kibbutz home and a lot of desert.

On the way back from Elat on the Red Sea, we stopped in Jerusalem again. Rick wanted to see the room where, according to legend, the Last Supper took place. We parked by the Jaffa Gate to the Old City, not thirty feet from a traffic cop. Good thing, we thought, because our rental car had no trunk. Our suitcases were mostly on the back seat.

We returned thirty minutes later to find the right rear window broken. All our luggage was gone except my golf clubs, still stuffed behind the rear seat, with about half of my clothes packed in its cover. Rick, seasoned traveler that he is, had left passport, credit cards, money, travelers checks, clothes — everything but his camera and the clothes he was wearing.

The traffic cop? Still there. If he had seen anything we don't know. He didn't speak English. We searched a vacant lot next to our parking spot and drove all around, hoping the thieves might have taken the money and pitched the rest. No luck. We went to the Jerusalem central police station to make a report, waited two hours until the only English speaking detective returned from dinner, and finally continued on to Tel Aviv, arriving around midnight.

Our Israeli tourism hosts were aghast, did everything but call out the army, and arranged for Rick to go to the U.S. Embassy the next day, a Saturday of course, where a vice-consul on her way to a tennis lesson met us to supply a letter so Rick could get back into the States.

I loaned him the $45 she charged, which we thought was a little much, as she asked Rick to give her parents a call when he got back to Detroit where they lived. It made for a very humorous column for his newspaper, but the parents weren't too thrilled to read it.

Rick swore I brought him bad luck.

To show you how soon we forget, Rick agreed to come to work for me ten years later.

Another lucky adventure I had with the Society of American Travel Writers led to an unscheduled "interview" with author James Michener, whom I had always admired for his unparalleled attention to detail — just like Walt. It happened in 1986, during our convention aboard the QE II as she sailed from New York to Southampton, and it was all a fortunate mistake.

Michener had been invited to join our cruise and address the society by his old friend and mine, Neil Morgan. Neil, one of the nation's best writers, was already known as the dean of San Diego columnists in 1952 when I moved to California. I met him at an SATW meeting in Brasilia. We share Walter Cronkite as a friend, among many others. Neil was the one who urged me to write this book of mental meanderings.

The QE II cruise was a remarkable cruise in many ways. There was a Force Ten gale most of the way. You had to hang on with both hands to stay in your bunk. The swimming pools were emptied. I was sure the stabilizers had gone haywire. Seasickness was not unknown.

Knowing this was the last steam cruise before going into dry-dock for new diesel engines, half the crew had jumped ship in New York. The rookie replacements didn't know where anything was.

The samovar tipped over in the dining room. The elaborate ice carving went sliding across the floor at the Captain's Ball. NBC correspondent Edwin Newman's lectern turned over, spilling his notes on the floor. He went on talking about language while collecting his notes on hands and knees. A grand piano slid clear across the floor during the contralto's recital.

On the fourth day and first sunny morning, I went down to breakfast early. The dining room was tilting back and forth. First you were ten floors up, then you were staring at the surface of the ocean. There were only two hardy guests in the room — Jim Michener and I.

He looked lonely, so I went over and asked if I could sit down. He didn't know me from Tangaroa. We talked for an hour about everything under the sun: his travels, my travels, his book, my job at Disney World. Before the end of the conversation I thought he seemed a little strange.

Only then did I realize he thought I was a big city newspaper reporter who had requested an interview and arranged the date the night before by phone. He didn't know him by sight. I don't know why he didn't show. Seasick? But what an opportunity for me! Michener, however, must have thought, "This guy asks the silliest questions I have ever been asked in an interview." I never told him the truth.

Later, several of us played Trivial Pursuit with Jim and his wife, Mari. I lost.

I also got to rub shoulders, almost literally, with every U.S. president since Nixon, with kings, queens and princes and with other special guests from all over the world including King Hussein of Jordan and Britain's Prince Andrew — one of my more unusual tours.

It was in 1980, when Prince Andrew was serving his time with the Royal Navy aboard a cruiser making goodwill visits to U.S. ports. They had visited Pensacola, where the British tabloid press had tried to make a heavy romance out of his date with the sheriff's daughter. In such a context, the Prince was sometimes referred to as "Randy Andy."

The ship was on its way to Fort Lauderdale. I got a call from an Irish-born writer for *Orlando Magazine* asking for assistance in arranging a "secret visit" by the Prince. He said his friend, the British consul in South Florida, had promised him an exclusive story if he could pull it off without the British press knowing. They were following like royal hunting hounds.

Only at sea did Prince Andrew escape the media spotlight and he wanted to turn the focus on the ship's goodwill mission.

We arranged for a VIP Hostess, a security host and me to accompany the Prince. It was unusual for me to go on such a tour, but we needed someone to handle the press if they showed up. The Prince arrived around noon; we spent the rest of the day enjoying Magic Kingdom attractions. As far as I know, in a simple navy pea coat, he went entirely unrecognized. We went on the *Walt Disney World Railroad* and to *It's a Small World* and other attractions.

That night, with our young hostess in the lead, we went to dinner at the Lake Buena Vista Club — very out of the way — where Prince Andrew regaled us with tales of life in Buckingham Palace.

The tale I recall best is how he and his younger brother would place hard rolls on napkins in their laps, jerk quickly on the edges of the napkins and then gaze around innocently as the rolls went flying through the air. He demonstrated. We laughed.

As it happens, the very pretty blond VIP Hostess chosen for the assignment was a classmate of my daughter at Trinity Preparatory School and the daughter of an Episcopal minister. Unfortunately for those of us trying to escape publicity, the young lady's name was Candy – just too much of a rhyme for the tabloids to resist, once they discovered the Prince's whereabouts.

Randy Andy and Candy Escape to Disney World just had to be the headline.

The following morning the tour continued with all of us hoping the press would leave us alone for just another two hours. It was obvious the Prince was enjoying every minute of the visit. And it ended as planned just in time.

My office received calls from British reporters who had somehow been tipped and were on their way at top speed from Fort Lauderdale. The Prince's tour ended on time at noon. His car picked him up behind Main Street and slipped out the employee gate just as the horde of British reporters came running through the front gate.

I had to face them with the unwelcome news that the Prince had gone.

"What did he do?"

"Where did he go?"

"Who was with him?"

I gave them a straightforward rundown, the Prince's ride on *Space Mountain*, *Jungle Cruise*, *Haunted Mansion* and, of course, our royal Cinderella Castle, all the pertinent facts. When they learned his guide was named Candy, they rushed to the phones. Then I listened as they telephoned their stories, inventing all kinds of fictitious intimate details, trying their best to hint at intrigue and romance. British tabloids are wont to do that.

Years later, I watched from a distance as Andrew's estranged wife, Fergie, took their two daughters through Disneyland Paris on a much more heavily publicized tour with a horde of photographers in tow.

Many of our VIP hostesses and tour guides made lasting friendships, exchanging letters with families they had taken on tour. Tour guiding is among the most desired positions in the parks. Both men and women, who are picked for their personalities and good looks, vie for the position.

For many years, beginning with Disneyland's Tencennial, we picked a young cast member as the Disneyland Ambassador and another as the Walt Disney World Ambassador. Many of them were former tour guides. At first they were pretty young women. Later men were added and finally a mixed group of five was chosen to represent the parks in public appearances, on TV shows and in ceremonial events.

The first year was more like a Miss America beauty contest, but later selections were based on a broader range of talents and knowledge. These young people traveled around the world representing their fellow employees and the spirit of Disney. Many stayed to take important jobs in marketing and operations after their year as Ambassador.

The role became increasingly important after Walt's death, when we needed a spokesperson to make public appearances for the company. Many of our executives, I think, were hesitant to assume Walt's role. Pretty young people could pull it off without inviting comparisons with Walt.

The Ambassador program was another invention of my mentor Jack Lindquist, who later became President of Disneyland. Jack never failed to support my crazy ideas and came up with even more of his own.

At one point, Jack was in charge of a team to "sell" World Showcase to nations and companies in foreign lands, not an easy job because we were seeking millions of dollars in participant fees. From the beginning, major corporations had seen the advantage of "sponsoring" major attractions in the park. Walt himself had recruited those companies when he was still alive, beginning with an old friend at the Santa Fe Railroad, along with Kodak, Coca-Cola, Pepsi and other companies who were sponsors of his television shows.

The New York World's Fair brought in sponsorship from General Electric (*Carousel of Progress*) that continued when that attraction moved to Disneyland and then to Disney World. RCA later joined in presenting *Space Mountain*. Some of the largest firms in the country became what we called *corporate alliance partners* in Epcot.

But selling World Showcase to foreign governments was a different matter. Many were used to sponsoring exhibits at World's Fairs for a year or even two. But committing for a ten-year contract created legal and budgetary problems for governments. In some cases, they wanted to produce the usual commercial displays about their manufacturing and agricultural industries. Disney designers wanted the showcases to be more entertaining and represent the recognizable landmarks, costumes and traditions of the country.

Except for Morocco, whose King signed on, national governments referred us to individual commercial organizations within their countries. We went ahead with a Circle-Vision 360 film on China because we had unexpectedly received permission from the Chinese government to do so, but with no government sponsorship. It is still the first place I take first-time visitors to Epcot and the film turns out to contain scenes of all the places I toured on my first trip to China in 2004. A Chinese importer in New York signed on to present the merchandise and restaurant in the pavilion. A major Japanese department store did likewise in Japan. Alliances were found for films in Canada and France.

Three of France's most famous chefs agreed to lease and run the restaurant there. Beck Beer sponsored Germany; Bass (the brewery) and Pringle (the woolen mills) did the same for the United Kingdom. Norway's pavilion was built in later years under a contract with Norwegian companies that had government backing.

While we were attempting to market the sponsorships, some government officials, looking at the designs we had created, objected that they did not truly represent their modern countries, where skyscrapers and glass-sided buildings dominate the cities. But our designers argued that all the pavilions would look alike if we adopted that theory.

Jack Lindquist frequently asked the Germans, for instance, if they were building a pavilion to represent the United States, what icons they would pick. Well, came the answer, Chicago gangsters and the Wild West. Enough said.

Disney Imagineers chose things like pyramids for Mexico, Munich city hall for Germany, the Imperial Palace for Japan and typical Parisian Belle Epoch architecture and a small version of the Eiffel Tower for France.

Lindquist made presentations to, among others, the Empress of Iran, who had frequently visited Walt Disney World, and to Imelda Marcos in Manila, both of whom held cultural posts in their governments at the time. Other Disney officials were invited to make presentations to the Soviet government in Moscow, but soon got bogged down in governmental red tape.

In the end, we built showcases for Mexico, China, Germany, Italy, Morocco, Japan, France, the United Kingdom and Canada plus the American Adventure in time for the 1982 opening. Each of them was, I think, successful in creating for guests the adventure of traveling in the country, enjoying its food and getting a sense of its culture.

In each pavilion, young people are brought for a one-year tour to represent each nation, as a part of the World Showcase Fellowship Program. They are selected from among candidates who still live in their native land, so they are familiar with their countries as they are today. They are universally bright young people, many just out of school, many interested in the hospitality industry as a career.

It gives our guests and cast a rare opportunity to meet the people of each of these countries and get a sense of being there. The international cast members come from all sides of the world, work in the Showcase earning money and spend one day a week in classes learning Disney operations. They learn about all our divisions and live in apartments near the property.

Instead of dividing the fellows into national groups, they are mingled. Usually three people live in an apartment, each from a different nation. They organize group dinners. One night China will cook, next time France. They get to know Disney and they get to know each other.

The young people cannot stay after their Fellowship tour, but must return to their native lands at the end of the year to be replaced by a new group. They try to keep track of us and each other when they leave. More than a few romances have developed over the years.

One involved the Englishman who later replaced me as head of publicity when I retired. In the early 1980s, he was a serving host in the United Kingdom's British pub. He married a very pretty fellowship student from a well-connected Mexican family who was working at World Showcase's Mexico. Duncan Wardle made up his mind after surveying all the divisions of the company that he wanted my job some day when I retired. With talent and ambition, he began working in our London office helping to market Walt Disney World and Disneyland.

I worked with him during the year I was at Disneyland Paris, when he was helping spread the word on the new park then under construction. Later, when I was in the process of retiring — it took a few years — he let my boss, Marketing Vice President Linda Warren, know he was interested and he got the job. He moved back to Orlando with his wife and children. Duncan moved up to be Vice President of International Marketing and, most recently, Vice President of Public Relations at Disneyland. Now there is a full circle for you.

My best friend and, I like to pretend, "my pupil" was and is John Dreyer. He ran the department at Walt Disney World while I was in France. Then, when I was preparing for retirement, he moved up to be Senior Vice President of Corporate Communications in California, working directly with Michael Eisner for many years.

As I look back after spending half my life with Disney, I realize that I lived through a revolution in technology, in music, in public attitudes and a shrinking of the world through jet transportation and space flights. It truly became a small world, although far different from the colorful attraction of that name that Walt created.

I witnessed the creation of eleven Disney parks, two Downtown Disneys, thirty hotels, two campgrounds and four water parks in the U.S., Japan, France and China. I wrote press releases about all of them and was there for most of those openings.

It kept me busy and moving fast. In fact, I got a reputation among my co-workers for fast driving and I blame it all on dinosaur fever.

When the dinosaurs Disney created for the New York World's Fair were brought back to California, they went to WED for refurbishing and then were brought to Disneyland on flatbed trailer trucks. We arranged to have them left uncovered so we could photograph the giant figures coming down the Santa Ana Freeway. Charlie Nichols and I drove to Glendale to catch the beginning of the run. Then, we would race ahead to a bridge crossing over the freeway for a photographic vantage point.

Charlie would grab the shot and jump back in the car as we tried to beat the rolling brontosaurus to another bridge. We had to get there in time to zip up an off ramp, stop and get set. Charlie was shooting a speed graphic with four-by-five film holders, which have to be reversed with each shot. That takes time.

The flatbeds were rolling along, probably about forty-five miles an hour, so we had to race at seventy to get ahead. It frequently took five miles or more the get far enough ahead to give Charlie time to set up. Charlie kept yelling, "Slow down!" but I was in a fever, hot to get the shots.

It was several months before I could convince him that this was a one-time race and he could ride with me safely. I think he warned all the others who might have thought about riding with me.

For the first fifteen years I had the best office location in Walt Disney World — overlooking Town Square in the Magic Kingdom. I could watch the people and the parades every day. I could even duck through my window onto a balcony for an unobstructed view. There was only one other office with that kind of view. Many operations, merchandising, food and entertainment division offices were located above the stores on Main Street, but because of the false fronts to the buildings, there were no windows to look out of.

In those early days, as we had at Disneyland, we wanted to be where the press coming in could find us easily. At Disneyland we were moved several times — into a temporary trailer just behind Main Street, up over the Opera House opposite City Hall and then back to City Hall, but always handy to the entrance.

With the opening of Epcot, however, it became impossible to find a place that was handy to everywhere. For a while we tried a branch office in Epcot — first inside *Spaceship Earth* and then next to the stroller rental facility at the Main Entrance. But with the coming of the other parks, we decided to move in with the rest of Marketing at the Sun Bank Building in what is now called Downtown Disney.

It was not centrally located, but at least it was fairly easy to find. The Team Disney Building was built just down the road from there to house most of the administrative offices. (By then, we'd kind of given up big time on Walt's old idea of not spending money on office buildings.)

I was there until I left for France in 1991. Soon after I had returned, however, Marketing outgrew its Sun Bank space and moved to makeshift facilities in what had been a defunct shopping mall. It was way to hell and gone on U.S. 192, past where Disney's Animal Kingdom was about to be built.

After I left, Marketing got an entire five-story building to itself in the Celebration area. Carefully designed cubicles and private offices for the Media Relations Department are a far cry from that cramped little office in Disneyland City Hall or the wide-open, yell-across-the-room quarters we shared in Disney World's Magic Kingdom. The new quarters are in beautifully designed buildings, but don't have either the location or the quaint character of the earlier days. I still think seeing those characters parading by my window every day was a great inspiration for writing publicity — and a great place to receive press visitors.

There were many financial highs and lows over the years as the fortunes of Disney stock went up and down like a yo-yo. If I had known just when to buy and sell — and I certainly should have foreseen many of the moves — I could have run a thousand dollars from the time Disneyland opened with an opening price of $2 a share, to a billion dollars by the time I retired. But then I didn't have a thousand dollars to spare in 1955.

Walt and Roy had originally formed a separate company because they knew shareholders would not stand still for a venture as risky as Disneyland. When it became a success, its shares were exchanged for Walt Disney Productions stock. When I began work in 1963, the share price was up to $49. After splitting two or three times, it jumped from $125 to $225 a share by the time Walt Disney World opened and it split again soon after it was clear that the new resort would be a smash hit.

By 1973, it was at a new high. Now was the time to sell and I should have known. A representative of Gulf Oil, our official oil company at the time, came to warn us that a gasoline shortage was coming that would have a severe effect on tourism. I had a little stock from options granted us through the years, but I was too loyal, or dumb, to sell. Oh well, I probably would have gone to jail for insider trading. By 1974 the price was down to $19 a share, barely ten percent of its previous value.

We began all kinds of publicity to counteract the effect of the 1973 gas shortage, which was really only serious in spots around the country. Strangely, it always seemed to be in high-profile locations like Miami, New York, Los Angeles or Chicago. I remember going to Michigan on one of my press missions when papers were full of the long gas lines in Miami and Orlando. There was plenty of gas between Detroit and Grand Rapids.

We instituted a hot line so guests could call and get accurate info on where gas was available. And we started reaching for hometown news stories to spread the word that the gas situation was not as bad as the national media was making it seem.

When our twenty-millionth guest was due to arrive, I remember going out to the parking lot, spotting a Wisconsin license plate — the farther the better — and following the guest to the front gate, where she was promptly selected as the honored twenty millionth guest, proving in the picture released to northern papers that you could get to Florida from the Midwest.

Attendance and our stock gradually recovered over the coming years, but by then Disney motion pictures were running into troubles at the box office. The company was threatened with various takeovers. Even with the opening of Epcot and the big attendance boost it created, Wall Street wasn't too happy with us. Not until Roy E. Disney stepped back into an active role in the company and the resultant hiring of Michael Eisner and Frank Wells as Chief Executive Officer and Chief Operating Officer respectively did our market fortunes rebound.

Now was definitely the time to buy. And I should have known that, too, but I was always afraid of the stock market anyway and stood on the sidelines while the stock and Disney reputation soared, went up and split two for one, went back up and split three for one. Some of my newspaper friends who bought stock after seeing Walt Disney World under construction were gleeful then, but if they held on into 1974, slightly mad at me. Those who bought in the mid-eighties thought we were wonderful. After 2001 and 9/11, however, they were unhappy with me again when the stock and tourism tumbled.

I have always been amused at the predictions and reactions of my friends among the business reporters, beginning with the *Mirror-News* writer who predicted dismal failure for Disneyland. In October 1971, they were writing about the disappointing opening at Walt Disney World. By Christmas, they were extolling its spectacular success.

But in February 1972, before the beginning of the winter tourist season, a *Business Week* reporter spent a week in Orlando listening to merchants groan about the slow time. He said the initial success might have been short lived. He wrote about suspicions that Disney World might not be the boon it had seemed in the fall.

Orlando Mayor Carl Langford, however, was more upbeat.

"Any mayor," he said, "would give his eye teeth to have Walt Disney World on his doorstep."

Carl was known as a plain-spoken guy around town. In describing his city to *Business Week* he said, "Orlando is the kind of town that used to keep the cottage cheese in the gourmet section at the supermarket."

He was right. The "City Beautiful" I found when I switched from Disneyland to Walt Disney World was definitely behind the growth curve I had seen in Orange County, California.

In Florida's Orange County, the pace was a lot slower. If the hardware store was out of hose connections you could expect the stock to be replaced the next time the plumbing salesman came around, whenever that would be.

There were two relatively new malls in town and a Jordan Marsh store, but the selection was so limited we made annual trips to Atlanta to get the kids school clothes.

Now there are giant malls all over town and the two that were there in 1971 are gone. There are Target Stores, Wal-Marts, Home Depots and Lowe's all over town. There are hundreds of restaurants, a couple hundred golf courses and recently some of the nations biggest department stores — Macy's, Saks, Nieman-Marcus and Bloomingdale's.

There must be five to ten hotels for each of the big chains like Holiday Inn, Hilton, Sheraton and Marriott — well over one hundred twenty thousand hotel rooms where just five thousand existed pre-Disney. At Walt Disney World alone, more than thirty thousand hotel rooms are well occupied where only fifteen hundred existed on opening day.

The kind of growth I witnessed in Orange County, California, in the fifties and sixties came with double impact to Orange County, Florida, in the eighties and nineties and it continues to this day.

Traffic gets congested regularly on I-4 in downtown Orlando, but I think no worse than when I came thirty years ago. The freeway and numerous toll roads have been expanded many times, barely keeping up with the demand.

Although Disney frequently gets the blame for the congestion, strangely, the jams are heaviest during the school year when there are the fewest tourists around, and lightest in the summer when millions are here. Most of the tourists are concentrated in the area south of town between International Drive and Walt Disney World, but traffic usually flows pretty well.

Air transportation is many times better than it was. When I came, Orlando was using a part of the U.S. Air Force B-52 base at McCoy Field. The airport is still coded MCO, but is now known as Orlando International Airport. Instead of a makeshift quonset hut left over from World War II, there is a huge modern terminal, in my estimation, one of the prettiest and most efficient I have ever used, and that's saying a lot. One of my former publicists has been PR director of the airport for fifteen years.

Chapter 22

*D*isney gets blamed for a lot of things around Orlando, mostly related to traffic and growth. I remember the first PR man I met when I came to town was Ed Cottrell at Martin-Marietta (now Lockheed Martin), which had moved a plant to Orlando in 1958.

"I'm sure glad Disney is here," he said. "Now the papers have someone else to blame for all the problems."

Over the years we have campaigned for better roads in the immediate surrounding area, supported bed taxes on hotel rooms to help build the Orange County Civic Center and boost area tourism, and worked with community leaders to solve other transportation problems in Central Florida.

As company spokesmen, as well as publicists, my staff and I were the ones to answer questions on political issues, accidents, emergencies or controversies, until recent years when an entire public relations department was organized to do the spokesman chore. We tried to answer directly and truthfully. I never had one of our executives complain that I had said the wrong things, even if I had. Sometimes they advised me. Sometimes I just knew what to say.

One of our early problems was with Highway 535, the one used by most cast members to reach a main employee parking lot near our back entrance. They were bused on our own roads from there to their jobs. The narrow county highway was dangerous with many sharp curves. Accidents piled up. With Dick Nunis leading the way, employees campaigned publicly to widen and straighten the highway. A pair of folk singers who were popular entertainers in the lounge of the Polynesian Village wrote and recorded a song, "Stay Alive on 535."

County Commissioners pleaded lack of funds for the job. They were also concerned with urban sprawl, shortage of schools, sewer lines, and other essential infrastructure. They placed a moratorium on multi-family developments and limited development to large lots. It was not until the 1990s that development in the area sky-rocketed.

The 535 campaign fizzled. Improvements came slowly. It was nearly twenty years before the highway was completely widened and realigned. With utility infrastructure and other major road improvements completed, development in the area skyrocketed.

Sometimes I got caught in the middle. One of our attorneys, who had played a major role in purchasing the property, was pushing a plan to build apartments for our employees a short distance from our property. He called and asked me to issue a news release announcing the project.

I had a suspicion, so I called Donn Tatum, then chairman of the Walt Disney board, and checked. No way. Hold on. Infrastructure problems were unsolved. The project was never announced.

Law enforcement was another issue in 1971. Then Sheriff David Starr of Orange County was sure his deputies, armed as usual, would be needed to patrol the streets of the Magic Kingdom to control the vast crowds "that were sure to come." Who knew how many criminals were among them?

Based on our experience at Disneyland, we knew better. We knew that our kind of friendly security presence created a uniquely safe and friendly atmosphere. Ours carried radios but no weapons. Even Secret Service agents carry their weapons hidden when they are in the park with Presidents and such.

Agreement was soon reached with the Sheriff's department for a regular liaison to provide assistance in case of a criminal activity that required arrest or incarceration.

❦

As the biggest game in town, Disney World always got more than its share of attention from local reporters. It was almost a game trying to figure out where they were getting some of the stories. With thousands of employees — five thousand in the beginning, with more than fifty-four thousand cast members now — there was never a shortage of rumors. Some were true, but some of the local newspaper stories were hard to fathom.

One seemed to me slightly ridiculous. "Investigative" Reporter Rob Johnson was new in town and assigned to the "Disney beat" for the *Sentinel*. Unlike any other local reporters through the years, Rob seemed to have it in for Disney. Some stories were pure speculaton with little or no foundation. Others seemed to exaggerate just to embarrass.

One was really far fetched. In 1967, the legislature created the Reedy Creek Improvement District with authority to supervise building codes, utilities, fire department and so forth on our property, in order that we could create a unique community in line with Walt Disney's concept of EPCOT, the experimental prototype community of tomorrow. It was supported solely by taxes on the Disney site.

Among other provisions, the District could build various kinds of energy plants including the gas powered electric plants that now provide a part of Disney's energy needs. It included the possibility of a small nuclear plant. The provision was written at a time when nuclear power was seen as "the wave of the future." By the time of Johnson's stories, however, following the Three Mile Island nuclear accident and other incidents, the whole idea of such a plant, even a small one, was out of the question.

Rob's story, pure speculation, implied that Disney was secretly planning such a plant at Bear Island where our sewage treatment plant was located. He made it sound like Bear Island was another Three Mile Island. Nothing I could say would change his mind.

Soon after, Rob authored another story about our problems with sewage disposal at a time when we were working with University of Florida environmental experts to experiment with new ways of filtering treated effluent by running it into the swamp around Reedy Creek. We hoped to find a better way to treat sewage effluent, which could then be adopted by other municipalities.

It worked in early tests, but then ran afoul of newly changed EPA rules, resulting in a small fine. Then several buzzards that had become a nuisance invading our bird sanctuary on Discovery Island died accidentally while being corralled for transfer to uninhabited forests. Record keepers had failed to obtain the proper permits for the move. We acknowledged our employees' errors and took extensive measures to prevent future problems.

The resulting stories seemed to exaggerate the negative. Johnson left the paper before long, the only local reporter I ever felt treated us badly.

I also got an angry complaint from one of the *Sentinel*'s editors-in-chief who called me at midnight, after I had turned down a request from the city desk — a demand that I go look up the personnel records of an employee who had been the victim of an apparent homicide. It didn't happen anywhere near Disney World. I didn't even know how to do such a thing at that time of night and couldn't have done so anyway because of privacy policies. Fortunately, he left a few months later. I also got in trouble with the local paper for a short time when ex-president Nixon came on a private visit. At the request of his Secret Service men, I didn't call the paper. Oh well.

Preconceived journalism was a frequent and sometimes amusing occurrence. I remember one instance when the *New York Times* had done a story in early December about Miami hoteliers who complained that reservations for the coming tourist season were way down. They were expecting a bad year for Florida tourism.

Two weeks later — network newsmen always seemed to follow up on *New York Times* or *Washington Post* stories — a CBS correspondent called to say he was coming in to do a story about the decline in Florida tourism. By the time he arrived we were into our busiest period of the year, Christmas season.

The reporter walked out on Main Street. The street was jammed with guests.

"Where did all the people come from?" he asked.

I told him it was a pretty normal crowd for the time of year. He should have come earlier if he wanted to see fewer.

He called New York, told them what was happening.

"Sorry, that's not the story we sent you for," they said. "Come on home."

The opening of Disney-MGM Studios gave us new opportunities for contacts with top editors and with television news people. We had great fun with groups like the *Time-Life* editors who held their annual editors' retreat at Disney World. We greeted them on the Studios backlot with shrieking "fans" begging for autographs and snapping pictures, making the editors feel like Hollywood celebrities. Our extras were good.

We had the Academy of Television Arts and Sciences Hall of Fame Awards at the Studios park for several years, giving me the chance to renew friendships with Walter Cronkite and other newsmen. That also brought performances by Bob Hope, George Burns and many others, many of whom are no longer with us.

One of our biggest publicity coups came when ABC's *Primetime* arranged to have Diane Sawyer interview Warren Beatty via satellite at the premiere for *Dick Tracy* held at the Studios park. Beatty was told he would not be asked any embarrassing questions about a recent fracas in Hollywood. (I don't remember exactly what it was.) First, the interview was begun, not by Diane, but unexpectedly by Sam Donaldson. Second, it was not about *Dick Tracy*, but about the embarrassing incident. Beatty immediately walked away. The interview was over.

✤

Network television frequently covered our openings and special events, particularly *Today, Good Morning America* and *CBS Morning News.* Their anchors and reporters became Disney friends, including Joan Lunden, Charlie Gibson, Katie Couric, Willard Scott, Paula Zahn and Harry Smith.

Paula came back one year to read the Christmas Story for the annual Candlelight Processional, or simply "Candlelight," as it was known. Walter Cronkite was another of my media friends who agreed to be the celebrity narrator for the Christmas event. Many of the narrators were Hollywood celebrities. I got to meet them because they always donned their robes in my office at City Hall. I rode back from California on an airplane with Cary Grant the year he was narrator. Gregory Peck, Perry Como, Rock Hudson, Joe Campanella, Dean Jones, and McLean Stevenson were among many others.

We never publicized the event because there was never enough room for the public to see it. The performance occurred on only one night a year as a kickoff to the Christmas season. By the time we got eight hundred singers on risers, several hundred invited community leaders and the relatives of the singers into Town Square and all the way down Main Street in front of the Railroad Station, there was no more room.

Similar events were held annually at Disneyland. Christmas never started for me until the night of Candlelight.

In later years, in order to accommodate thousands of guests, the event was moved to Epcot's America Gardens Theatre and held every night for two weeks with a different celebrity narrator each night. The processional is spectacular but somehow lacks the cozy feeling of the Town Square in the Magic Kingdom.

Many of those nights were the first chilly night of the year. We had to give out blankets to guests seated in Town Square. Several times, it started to mist as if by magic. Coming through the spotlight beams, the drizzle looked like snow. Christmas was here. Candlelight was another of those very special events that originated in the fertile imagination of Walt Disney.

Another of the annual Christmastime events at Disneyland was the visit of the Rose Bowl teams. They came in blazers so they could be recognized and had a ball on the attractions for the afternoon. They finished the tour with a huge prime rib dinner in the park. For a time we had a contest to see which team could down the most beef. We gave it up when coaches decided their players were getting "beef-logged."

One year, when the *WEDWAY PeopleMover* was brand new, the Purdue University team was stuck for an hour on the trackway twenty feet above Tomorrowland. Not very good publicity. We were a little frantic and the coach was afraid his players would catch cold as darkness descended. Fortunately, it ended well when the ride restarted smoothly.

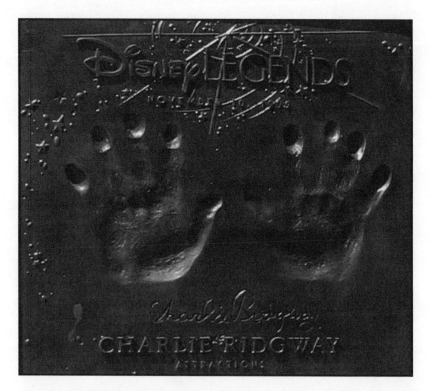

It's not Grauman's Chinese Theater, but to me it's even more special. This plaque, with my hand prints in bronze, is permanently displayed in the courtyard of the Team Disney-Michael D. Eisner Building at Walt Disney Studios.

Chapter 23

When I was offered the Disneyland job, I spent many sleepless nights debating whether I wanted to leave the news business for publicity. I told my newspaper friends this was probably the only PR job in the world I could stomach for more than a few weeks. I was right! I have trudged across the construction sites of all eleven Disney parks in the U.S., France, Japan and China, ruined more than one pair of shoes walking through sand and mud and bruised at least three sets of springs on my cars — and I loved every minute of it.

I spent a day in Tokyo Disneyland when it was only half-built. I got to know intimately the two parks in Disneyland Paris plus the four main parks, thirty hotels and three water parks in Florida, and two parks and two hotels in Anaheim. I spent a day at Hong Kong Disneyland eighteen months before opening and then spent two weeks toward the end of construction writing a Media Guide for the opening. It looked just like the original Disneyland exactly fifty years before — castle hiding behind scaffolding and all. That certainly brought back a flood of memories.

There is always one special moment when I go back to any of Walt's Magic Kingdoms — when I walk into Town Square and look down Main Street to the Castle and listen to the little ones shouting, "Look Mom, there's the castle!" Walt would like that.

Disney castles may be the world's most photographed icons — more visitors than the Palace of Versailles or mad King Ludwig's

German castle that inspired Walt originally. Disneyland Paris, which has its own queen-size Sleeping Beauty Castle, has three times as many visitors as any European castle or even the Eiffel Tower. Tokyo Disneyland has higher attendance than any of the other three Disney Magic Kingdoms.

What made Walt choose it as the symbol of fantasy? I wish I knew, but it is just one more mark of his genius. He had wanted Disneyland's castle to be big enough that you could see it driving down the highway approaching the park. In Walt Disney World and France, that vision was realized — too late for Walt to see.

In recent years, when young cast members at Walt Disney World spotted my Mickey Mouse Ring with the 1963 date, they looked at me like I was related to Methuselah. I didn't have the heart to tell them I had four careers before Disney.

And always — the first question they asked was, "Did you know Walt? What kind of a guy was he?"

Well gang, I never had time to answer that fully, because as you can see above, it takes a while. All I usually had time to say was, "He was a hell of a guy. Whenever you spent time with Walt, you knew that you had been with a unique person."

He was not overwhelming, not a great speaker and at first glance not a giant force. He was warm, human, full of ideas and energy, enthusiastic, someone you wanted to spend the day or a week or a year with, just watching and listening. I never talked intimately with Walt about anything except work, but my memories of him are as strong as ever. I still feel he was a real friend. So do many people who never saw him except on television. No one but a true genius could have such a lasting effect on the people who knew him, the people who only heard about him, and on the world at large.

I have known billionaires and great writers, actors and celebrities, presidents and princes, but none can compare with Walt.

When it opened, Disneyland still had several unfinished attractions. Asked when it would be finished, Walt replied, "Disneyland will never be completed. It will continue to grow as long as there is imagination left in the world."

Of Walt Disney World he said, "There's enough land here to hold all the ideas and plans we can possibly imagine."

Well, Walt, maybe not — because Disney imagination now stretches to parks and motion picture and television entertainment around the world and there is much more to come. But no one needs to worry. There always seems to be plenty of imagination still inspired by Walt Disney to go around.

For me the past half century has been exciting, entertaining and more rewarding than I could have imagined in 1955, when I first saw Disneyland, or 1963, when I started working there.

One of the most gratifying rewards came when I was named a "Disney Legend," with a plaque in the courtyard of what's now renamed the Michael D. Eisner Building at Walt Disney Studios. There, huge statues of the Seven Dwarfs support the roof and look down on the Legends' courtyard.

I know I don't belong in the company with Julie Andrews, Tim Allen, Mary Costa, Annette Funicello, Buddy Ebsen and all the other stars who contributed so much to the Disney legend, but I am proud to be there with names like Dick Nunis, Card Walker, Bill Evans, Eddie Meck, Wathel Rogers, Marty Sklar, Jack Lindquist and so many more friends who made joy out of my Disney days.

I'm also pleased that six of my European "guides" are among the Legends. They were the Disney merchandising men who took me in hand in my first trips to Europe, finding the right editors for me to meet, arranging my hotels, giving me the confidence to travel afar, making it easy.

By coincidence, I was at Disneyland Paris the day they were given their Legend Awards by Michael Eisner and Roy E. Disney. Other awards that day went to Sir John Mills and many other celebrated European actors and filmmakers who contributed to the Disney legend. Mighty fine company for a simple press agent!

❧

Even more important to me is a special window on the second floor, just above the "Arcade" doorway on Main Street, U.S.A. — a window with gold-leaf lettering. After I left Disneyland, Eddie Meck retired. They gave him a window with his name displayed above that other Main Street. Windows in both parks display vintage signs as if they were real offices for contractors, tailors, lawyers and so forth.

Walt's father's name is there as "Elias Disney, Contractor." But most names belong to those who helped build the parks, including Imagineers, merchandise and operations people.

At Walt Disney World, Jack Lindquist's name appears as purser for the Peterson Travel Agency, upstairs at the corner of Main and Center streets. "Exclusive Agency for the Titanic," it reads. According to other window signs, Dick Nunis runs a massage parlor, Roy and Patty Disney and their four children run a sailmaking business (Roy is a great sailing enthusiast), and Ron and Diane Miller and their seven children are proprietors of Lazy M Ranch. They really are. Most of the window decorations were put up when the park opened in 1971.

By 1998, when I was ready to take life a little easier, there were not many vacant windows left. I actually retired in 1993, but continued working as a full-time consultant for another five years. Few people noticed the change in status. Many others were retiring, but very few new windows appeared. It took an okay from the highest level.

To a few close friends, I confided my long-time yearning for a window like Disneyland's Eddie Meck. Someone must have whispered in Michael Eisner's ear. Not only was there a new window but a mini-parade accompanied the unveiling. Michael and Mary Poppins were on hand for the unveiling, along with veteran staff members, my most cherished friends. In gold letters the sign reads:

Ridgway Public Relations
Charles Ridgway Press Agent
No Event Too Small

Okay. So call me sentimental. See if I care.

Epilogue

$\mathscr{S}$ome readers may wonder why I have ignored the turbulent controversy between Michael Eisner, Roy E. Disney, and current members of Walt Disney Company management and board of directors during the past few years.

Frankly, my intimate knowledge of company management in the last five years is happily very limited and very second hand. I would much rather remember those glory days when Michael and Frank Wells were producing extraordinary Disney magic, building Disney-MGM Studios, Disneyland Paris Resort and Tokyo DisneySea, plus some of the world's grandest new architectural icons. At the same time, they produced such phenomenal motion picture classics as *The Little Mermaid*, *Aladdin*, *Beauty and the Beast* and *The Lion King* — animated features that matched the best ever produced by Walt Disney.

Michael and Frank together created the second greatest joined-at-the hip executive I ever hope to know — second only to Walt himself. From the day they took over in 1984, the excitement, creativity and joy of working for Disney were just what they had been in Walt's lifetime.

In terms of pure architectural grandeur, including the new parks, more than twenty spectacular new hotels and imaginative outdoor recreation facilities, the Eisner-Wells accomplishments, in my view, were right up there with the Taj Mahal and Versailles. There's nothing to match them in modern times except Walt's own Magic Kingdoms.

Secondly, both Michael and Roy Disney were extraordinarily kind to me, truly inspiring, good bosses and good friends. So I refuse to take sides. Michael and Jane, Roy and Patty were almost like family, sharing wonderful experiences even at a distance. Roy and I share memories going back at least fifty years, including exciting times with Walt Disney himself. I shared with Michael energy-filled meetings, information-filled walking tours, creative conversations and rare inspiration on two continents for more than twenty years.

Michael was criticized in recent years for micro-managing, taking part in every little decision. I am very certain that Walt himself was the greatest micro-manager of all. And he constantly proved that his insistence on attention to every little detail and quality above all, with cost-cutting second, was the way to greater success and, ultimately, greater profit.

Anyhow, it was a lot more fun working at Disney when Walt or Michael was working with us, "micro-managing" every little detail. It has always been *details* that made the Disney parks unique. If I needed proof, it is what I heard constantly from my news-media friends who came to Disney parks and to our extravagant press parties —

"Nobody does it like Disney."

Remember how I said nostalgia strikes a chord with people? Well, 2005 turned out to be a year of extraordinary nostalgia for me, going back in memory to the opening of Disneyland and beyond.

I drove through East Central Germany from Frankfurt to Dresden over the identical route I rumbled along in a noisy, olive drab U.S. Army half-track vehicle exactly *sixty years before*.

I made a driving trip *back sixty-five years* to the sleepy farming area around the timeless little town of Shelbina in northeast Missouri where I spent the last two years of high school, a major move after spending my life up to that time in metropolitan areas of Chicago and Washington, D.C. I was able to find the Victorian farmhouse where we lived with no electricity; what little remained of my father's birthplace crossroads of Maud, Missouri, now just two houses and a tiny country church; and the high school where my mother and father met ninety-five years ago in nearby Paris, Missouri.

My nostalgic journeys turned three-dimensional when I flew to Hong Kong for one more Disney publicity chore, writing the Media Guide for the then nearly finished Hong Kong Disneyland. There I was, as I had been *fifty years before* and half a world away, walking down a muddy Main Street, U.S.A. and standing in front of a fairytale castle still half-hidden by scaffolding.

But the strangest nostalgic discovery came on my way back from China. I spent three days in Anaheim during the beginning of Disneyland's Fiftieth Anniversary celebration *on May 5, 2005.* I attended Disney Legends ceremonies where many of the new honorees were friends I had met in 1963 during the first weeks of my Disney career.

Coincidental nostalgia struck for a final time when I unearthed a copy of that first newspaper story I wrote about David Potthast's "sneak peak" at the new Disneyland. The date on the clipping — *May 5, 1955.*

Index